MONEY · MOON · MUMMY · MUSIC · MYTHOLOGY · NASCAR · NATURAL DISASTERS · NORTH AMERICAN INDIAN · OCEAN

OIL · OLYMPICS · PERSPECTIVE · PHOTOGRAPHY · PIRATE · PLANT · POND & RIVER · PREHISTORIC LIFE · PRESIDENTS

PYRAMID · RELIGION · RENAISSANCE · REPTILE · RESCUE · ROBOT · ROCKS & MINERALS · RUSSIA · SEASHORE

SHAKESPEARE · SHARK · SHELL · SHIPWRECK · SKELETON · SOCCER · SOLDIER · SPACE EXPLORATION · SPORTS

SPY · SUBMARINE · SUPER BOWL · TECHNOLOGY · TEXAS · TIME & SPACE · TITANIC · TRAIN · TREASURE

TREE · UNIVERSE · VAN GOGH · VIETNAM WAR · VIKING · VOLCANOES & EARTHQUAKES · VOTE · WATER · WATERCOLOR

WEATHER · WHALE · WILD WEST · WITCHES & MAGIC-MAKERS · WORLD SERIES · WORLD WAR I · WORLD WAR II

Eyewitness
Universe

Hubble Space Telescope

High-energy particle tracks

Magellan Venus orbiter

Jupiter and its moon Io

Martian Volcano

The surface of Mars

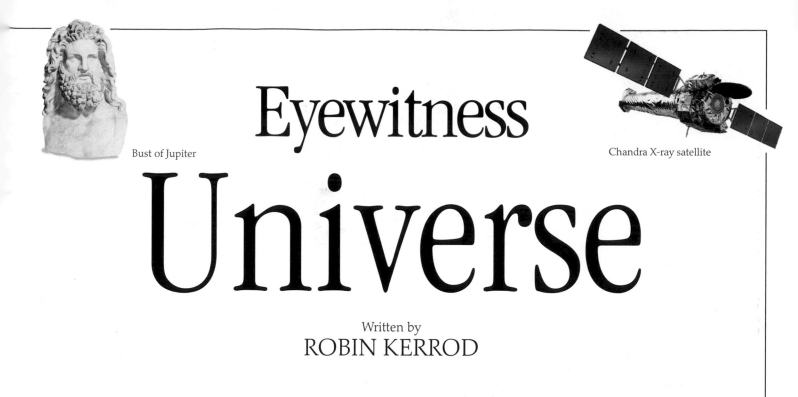

Bust of Jupiter

Chandra X-ray satellite

Eyewitness
Universe

Written by
ROBIN KERROD

DK Publishing

Core of a quasar

Mars

DK

LONDON, NEW YORK,
MELBOURNE, MUNICH, AND DELHI

Project editor Giles Sparrow
Art editor Tim Brown
Senior editor Kitty Blount
Senior art editor Martin Wilson
Managing editor Andrew Macintyre
Managing art editor Jane Thomas
Category Publisher Linda Martin
Art director Simon Webb
Production Erica Rosen
Picture research Sean Hunter
DTP Designer Siu Yin Ho

REVISED EDITION
Consultant Carole Stott
Editors Jayne Miller, Steve Setford
Art editors Edward Kinsey, Peter Radcliffe
Managing editor Camilla Hallinan
Managing art editor Owen Peyton Jones
Art director Martin Wilson
Associate publisher Andrew Macintyre
Production editors Laragh Kedwell
Production controller Pip Tinsley
Picture research Myriam Megharbi

This Eyewitness ® Guide has been conceived by
Dorling Kindersley Limited and Editions Gallimard

First published in the United States in 2003
This revised edition published in 2009 by DK Publishing,
375 Hudson Street, New York, New York, 10014

Copyright © 2003, © 2009 Dorling Kindersley Limited

09 10 11 12 13 10 9 8 7 6 5 4 3
ED775 – 03/09

A catalog record for this book is available from
the Library of Congress.

ISBN 978-0-7566-5030-8 (Hardcover)
ISBN 978-0-7566-5031-5 (Library Binding)

Color reproduction by Colourscan, Singapore
Printed by Toppan Co. (Shenzen) Ltd., China

Discover more at
www.dk.com

Spectroscope

Earth

Sunrise at Stonehenge

Very Large Array
radio telescope

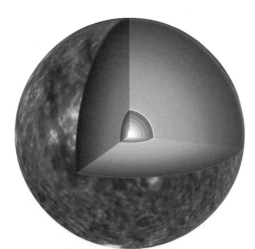
Inside a supergiant star

Interior of Jupiter

Contents

What is the universe?

THE UNIVERSE IS EVERYTHING THAT EXISTS—today, in the past, and in the future. It is the immensity of space, populated by innumerable galaxies of stars and permeated with light and other radiation. When we look up into the blackness of the night sky, we are peering deep into the fathomless depths of the universe. Although the stars we see are all trillions of miles away, they are actually close neighbors, because the universe is unimaginably vast. Humans have been fascinated with the starry heavens from the earliest times and have been studying them systematically for at least 5,000 years. But although astronomy is probably the oldest science, it has changed continually throughout its history.

SPACESHIP EARTH
The *Apollo 8* astronauts were the first people to see our planet floating alone in the universe, as they headed for the Moon in 1968. Other astronauts had remained too close to Earth to see the planet whole. It is Spaceship Earth, a beautiful, cloud-flecked azure world, which is the only place we know where there is life. Profoundly important to us Earthlings, no doubt, but completely insignificant in the universe as a whole.

"The history of astronomy is a history of receding horizons."

EDWIN HUBBLE
Discoverer of galaxies beyond our own

ANCIENT ASTRONOMERS
Ancient Britons were familiar with the regular movements of the Sun, Moon, and stars. In around 2600 BCE they completed Stonehenge. In its circles of huge megaliths and smaller standing stones, there were alignments that marked critical positions of the Sun and Moon during the year. Many other ancient monuments around the world also have astronomical alignments.

Sun orbits Earth

Earth at center of Ptolemaic universe

Babylonian astrological tablet

ASTROLOGY
The priests of ancient Babylon looked to the skies for good and bad signs that they thought might affect the people and matters of state. The idea that what happened in the heavens could affect human lives formed the basis of astrology, a belief that held sway for thousands of years and still has its followers even today.

PTOLEMY'S UNIVERSE
The last of the great classical astronomers, an Alexandrian Greek named Ptolemy, summed up the ancient concept of the universe in about 150 CE. The Ptolemaic universe had Earth at its center, with the Sun, Moon, and planets circling around it, within a sphere of fixed stars.

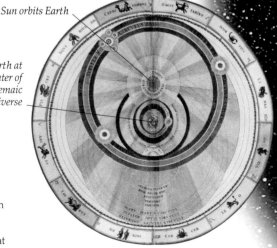

WORLD IN MOTION

Johannes Kepler
(1571–1630)

In 1543, astronomy was revolutionised when Nicolaus Copernicus put forward the idea of a Sun-centered universe. In the Copernican system, Earth and the other planets traveled around the Sun in circular orbits, but astronomers couldn't match the observed motions of the planets with this idea. Then German Johannes Kepler discovered why—the planets travel around the Sun, not in circles, but in ellipses. This discovery formed Kepler's first law of planetary motion.

Neptune *Saturn* *Earth* *Sun* *Mars* *Jupiter* *Uranus*

CELESTIAL CLOCKWORK

Kepler's laws of planetary motion explained precisely how the planets move. He likened what he called the "celestial machine" to clockwork and came close to fathoming the underlying cause, believing that the Sun must assert a magnetic force on the planets. In 1687, Isaac Newton finally explained why the planets orbit as they do, showing that gravity, not magnetism, is the fundamental force that holds the universe together.

Mechanical model (orrery) of the solar system

Hand-wound mechanism

STARS AND GALAXIES

Early astronomers visualized the stars as points on the inside of a great celestial sphere that enveloped Earth. By the late 1700s, astronomers were beginning to work out what our galaxy was really like. By plotting the distribution of stars, William Herschel proved that our galaxy was lens-shaped (it is, in fact, a bulging spiral). The existence of galaxies beyond our own was not proved until 1923, when Edwin Hubble discovered that the Andromeda "nebula" lay far beyond our home star system.

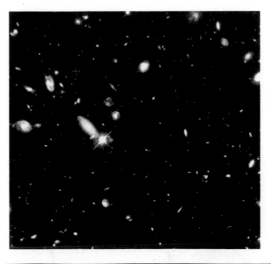

Andromeda is a spiral galaxy like our own

Stars in our own galaxy

The Andromeda Galaxy, M31

EVERYTHING'S RELATIVE

Early last century, a young German physicist named Albert Einstein transformed the way in which we look at space and the universe. He introduced his theories of relativity—the special theory in 1905 and the general theory 10 years later. One of the ideas presented in these theories is that nothing can move faster than the speed of light and that energy and mass are equivalent and can be converted into each other. Also, three-dimensional space and time are not separate entities, but are interrelated.

A field of galaxies whose light has taken up to 10 billion years to reach us

How do we fit in?

To us earthlings, our planet is the most important thing there is, and not very long ago, people thought our planet was the center of the universe. Nothing could be farther from the truth—in the universe as a whole, Earth is not the least bit special. It is an insignificant speck of rock circling a very ordinary star in an ordinary galaxy in one tiny corner of space. Exactly how big the universe is, no one really knows, but astronomers are now detecting objects so far away that their light has been traveling toward us for about 13 billion years. This puts them at a distance of some 76 sextillion miles (123 sextillion kilometers)—a distance beyond our comprehension.

Medieval world map

SMALL COSMOS
In medieval times, before the great voyages of discovery and exploration that began in the 15th century, people assumed that Earth was the whole universe. Many supported the idea of a flat Earth—go too far and you would fall over the edge.

SCALE OF THE UNIVERSE
Our insignificance in the universe as a whole is graphically portrayed in this sequence of images, from life at the human scale to the immeasurable immensity of intergalactic space. One way to help understand the scale of the universe is to consider how long it would take to travel from place to place, at the speed of light, 186,000 miles per second (300,000 km/s). Astronomers frequently use the light-year (5.9 trillion miles or 9.5 trillion km) as a measure of cosmic distances.

From space, Earth looks blue due to the vast expanses of surface water. White clouds surround the planet.

The Oort Cloud of icy, cometlike bodies forms an outer boundary around the whole solar system. It would take over a year and a half to reach the outer edge of the Oort Cloud at the speed of light.

Runners in a marathon cross a crowded bridge.

A satellite in orbit, hundreds of miles above Earth, looks down on the city.

OUR VIEW OF THE UNIVERSE
We look out at the universe from inside a layer of stars that forms the disk of our galaxy. We see the greatest density of stars when we look along the plane of this disk—in this direction the galaxy extends for tens of thousands of light-years. In the night sky, we see this dense band as the Milky Way. To either side of the Milky Way, we are looking through the disk, but this time perpendicular to its plane and see far fewer stars. By combining satellite images of the sky in all directions, we can capture an overall picture of what the universe looks like from inside our galaxy (left).

In the solar system, Earth lies three planets out from the Sun. It would take more than eight minutes to travel to the Sun at the speed of light.

While it would take only a few hundred thousand years to reach our closest galactic neighbors at light speed, most galaxies would require journey times of millions of years. The farthest ones would take billions of years to reach.

To reach the next nearest star would take over four years at the speed of light. Crossing the galaxy from edge to edge would take 100,000 years.

Venus

Earth

Jupiter

Saturn

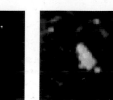
Uranus

Neptune

FAMILY PORTRAIT
Since the beginning of the Space Age, knowledge about our neighbors in space, the planets, has mushroomed. On a remarkable 12-year voyage of discovery, the *Voyager* probes visited all four giant planets—Jupiter, Saturn, Uranus, and Neptune. In 1990, *Voyager 1* looked back on its way out of the solar system and snapped a family portrait of six of the planets. They appear as little more than tiny specks lost in the vastness of space.

THE LOCAL UNIVERSE
Through the most powerful telescopes, astronomers can see galaxies in every direction they look. The picture above shows a plot of the positions of around two million galaxies in one region of space. Careful study shows that the galaxies are arranged in clusters and superclusters, which themselves form interconnecting sheets and ribbons around vast empty spaces, or voids—the large-scale structure of the cosmos.

How the universe works

THE UNIVERSE IS MADE UP of scattered islands of matter in a vast ocean of empty space. Energy travels through the universe in the form of light and other radiation. Fundamental forces and laws dictate what matter is like and how it behaves. The strongest of the four fundamental forces (the strong force) binds particles together in the nucleus of atoms. The weak and electromagnetic forces also act within the atom. Electromagnetism binds electrons to the nucleus; it also creates the phenomena of electricity and magnetism. Gravity is the weakest of the fundamental forces, but operates over the greatest distances to hold the universe together.

Water droplet

Water molecule consists of one oxygen and two hydrogen atoms

Protons have a positive electric charge

Inside atom, electrons orbit a tiny nucleus

Neutrons have no charge

Nucleus

Electrons have a negative electric charge

INSIDE ATOMS
The atoms that make up matter are not indivisible, as Democritus and Dalton thought. They are made up in turn of tinier, subatomic particles. The three main particles are protons, neutrons, and electrons. The protons and neutrons are found in the center, or nucleus, of an atom, while the electrons circle in orbits around the nucleus.

Protons and neutrons are made up of even tinier particles called quarks

ELEMENTS AND ATOMS
Greek philosopher Empedocles (around 490–430 BCE) believed matter was made up of four ingredients, or elements—fire, air, water, and earth. His fellow philosopher Democritus (around 460–370 BCE) thought instead that matter was made of tiny, indivisible parts he called atoms. His ideas were forgotten until English chemist John Dalton (1766–1844) laid the foundations of modern atomic theory in 1808. Matter is made of different chemical elements; each is unique because it is made up of different atoms.

Empedocles

Radio waves (wavelengths 1 mm or more)

Peak

Trough

Trough

Wavelength

A FAMILY OF WAVES
The radiation that carries energy through the universe takes the form of electric and magnetic disturbances that we call electromagnetic waves. There are many kinds of radiation, differing in wavelength—the distance between one peak or trough of the wave and the next. Visible light is radiation that our eyes can detect. It has wavelengths between 390 and 700 nanometers (nm) that we see as colors from violet to red (one nanometer is a billionth of a meter). There are invisible wavelengths shorter than violet light and longer than red. Gamma rays have wavelengths of fractions of a nanometer, while radio waves can be miles long.

Particle tracks at the European nuclear research center in Geneva

Similar poles of magnets repel each other

Iron filings reveal invisible lines of magnetic field

MAGNETISM
Magnetism is the force that makes magnets attract iron filings. The Earth has magnetism, too. When suspended, a magnet will align itself north-south, in the direction of our planet's magnetic field. Earth's magnetism extends far out into space, creating a bubblelike region called the magnetosphere. Other planets have powerful magnetic fields; so do the Sun and the stars.

PROBING THE ATOM
Physicists use incredibly powerful machines called particle accelerators, or "atom smashers," to investigate the structure of atoms. These machines accelerate beams of subatomic particles and smash them into atoms or other particle beams. The force of collision generates showers of subatomic particles, which leave trails of tiny bubbles in detectors called bubble chambers.

GRAVITY

English scientist Isaac Newton (1642–1727) established the basic law of gravity: that every body attracts every other body because of its mass. The more massive a body, the greater its gravitational attraction. With nearly 100 times the mass of Earth, Saturn has enormous gravity. Its pull keeps rings of particles circling around its equator and at least 60 moons in orbit around it. In turn, Saturn is held in the grip of the Sun's gravity, like all the planets. The Sun's gravity reaches out trillions of miles into space.

Saturn, its rings, and three of its satellites photographed by the Hubble Space Telescope

"The most incomprehensible thing about the world is that it is comprehensible."

ALBERT EINSTEIN

Infrared
(700 nm to 1 mm)

Ultraviolet
(10 nm to 390 nm)

X-rays
(0.001 nm to 10 nm)

Gamma rays
(up to 0.001 nm)

Visible light
(390 nm to 700 nm)

Europe's infrared observatory ISO

ISO view of Rho Ophiuchi star-forming region

THE HIDDEN UNIVERSE

With our eyes, we see the universe as it appears in visible light. But the universe gives out radiation at invisible wavelengths as well, from gamma rays to radio waves. We can study radio waves from the heavens with ground-based radio telescopes. Other invisible radiations can only be studied from space, using satellites. If we could see at other wavelengths, the universe would appear quite different.

ENERGY AND LIGHT

When you heat up an iron poker in a fire, its color changes, from gray to dull red, to bright red, and to yellow-white. As the temperature rises, the iron gives out shorter wavelengths (colors) of light. It is the same in space—the coolest red stars have a temperature of less than 5,500°F (3,000°C), while the hottest blue-white stars have temperatures more than 10 times greater. Even hotter, higher-energy objects emit mostly ultraviolet and X-ray radiation.

In the beginning

WE HAVE A GOOD IDEA of what the universe is like today and what makes it tick. But where did it come from? How old is it? How has it evolved? What will happen to it in the future? The branch of astronomy that studies and attempts to answer these questions is known as cosmology. Cosmologists think they know when and how the universe began and has evolved, although they are not so certain about how it might end (p. 14). They believe that an explosive event called the Big Bang, around 13.75 billion years ago, created the universe and started it expanding. Amazingly, cosmologists have figured out the history of the universe since it was one-ten-million-trillion-trillion-trillionth of a second old. It was at this time that the known laws of physics and the fundamental forces of nature came into being.

WHAT CAME BEFORE?
Nothing existed before the Big Bang—no matter, no space, no radiation, no laws of physics, no time. The birth of a baby marks the start of its independent life, in the same way that the Big Bang marks the start of time for the universe. But the baby was formed from its parents, whereas all the material of the universe was created in the Big Bang.

HOW THE UNIVERSE EVOLVED
The most drastic changes in the universe occurred in the first three minutes after the Big Bang. During this time, the temperature of the universe fell from countless trillion trillions of degrees to about a billion degrees. This dramatic cooling allowed the conversion of energy into subatomic particles, such as electrons, and hydrogen and helium nuclei. But it took a further 300,000 years before these particles combined to form atoms of hydrogen and helium, which would later seed the first galaxies.

ABBÉ GEORGES LEMAÎTRE
Around 1930, Georges Lemaître (1894–1966), a Belgian priest turned cosmologist, suggested the universe was created in a single moment when a "primeval atom" exploded. Matter was scattered into space and eventually condensed into stars and galaxies. Lemaître's ideas laid the foundation for the Big Bang theory.

Big Bang creates the universe, which is infinitely small, infinitely hot, and full of energy

Energy from the Big Bang creates particles of matter and antimatter, which annihilate one another

As the universe cools, combinations of particles become stable

A fraction of a second into its life, the universe expands to an enormous size in an event called inflation

As the universe cools down, quarks become the dominant type of matter

Quarks collide to form protons and neutrons, the particles found in atomic nuclei

Lightweight electrons and positron particles form

Matter too dense for light to travel freely

Light waves bounce off particles before traveling far, just as in a fog

Most electrons and positrons collide and annihilate each other

Universe expanding from Big Bang

Temperature drops through 5,500°F (3,000°C) and electrons are soaked up into atoms

Temperature is steadily dropping

Matter condenses to form galaxies and clusters

BECOMING TRANSPARENT
Until the universe was about 300,000 years old, it was full of particles and opaque. Then electrons began combining with atomic nuclei to form the first atoms, an event called decoupling. The fog of particles suddenly cleared, and radiation was able to travel long distances for the first time. The universe became transparent.

Photons now travel freely in largely empty space

Photons from the time of decoupling are the earliest we can hope to detect

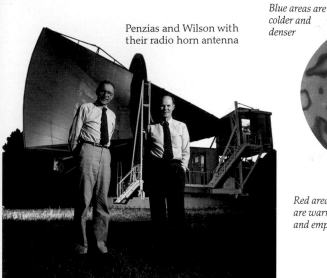

Penzias and Wilson with their radio horn antenna

Blue areas are colder and denser

Red areas are warmer and emptier

RIPPLES IN THE COSMOS
For the galaxies we see today to have formed, the universe must be "lumpy"—even at the earliest times, matter must have clumped together in certain areas. The COBE (Cosmic Background Explorer) satellite made the first accurate map of the radiation left over from the Big Bang (above). It shows slight variations in the background temperature that are believed to reflect the lumpiness in the early universe.

ECHOES OF THE BIG BANG
If the Big Bang really happened, physicists calculate that by now the temperature of the whole universe would have fallen to about 5.5°F (3°C) above absolute zero, -459°F (-273°C). In 1965, US physicists Arno Penzias and Robert Wilson picked up weak radio signals coming from all parts of the sky. They were equivalent to a cosmic background temperature of around -454°F (-270°C), providing convincing evidence for the Big Bang.

BOOMERANG
The joint US/European BOOMERANG project flew microwave instruments into the stratosphere around Antarctica in balloons. In 1998 and again in 2003, the balloons rode the winds that circle the South Pole. With their detectors cooled to a fraction of a degree above absolute zero, BOOMERANG mapped the microwave background with great precision.

A relatively small number of electrons survive

Protons and neutrons combine to form atomic nuclei

Electrons still unattached

Electrons combine with nuclei to form atoms

The universe as it is today, full of galaxies, stars, and planets, and still expanding

Universe still opaque. Pressure of radiation stops most matter from clumping together.

Universe becomes transparent

Matter starts to condense

Fate of the universe

EINSTEIN'S MISTAKE?
In 1917, when Albert Einstein (1879–1955) set out to describe the universe mathematically, he included a "cosmological constant"— an outward force to prevent the universe from collapsing. At the time he did not know that the cosmos is in fact expanding. His "mistaken" idea has recently been revived with the concept of dark energy.

THE BIG BANG CREATED THE UNIVERSE and started it growing, and it has been expanding ever since. But what will happen in the future— what is the ultimate fate of the cosmos? Will the universe expand forever, or will it one day stop expanding and endure a long, protracted cold death? Or, perhaps it will be ripped apart, or even shrink until it is squashed together in a reverse Big Bang. The answer depends on the density of the universe's matter and energy, and on the effect of dark energy. This unknown gravity-opposing force constitutes about 73 percent of the universe compared to atom-based matter such as stars and galaxies which makes up just four percent.

UNIVERSAL EXPANSION
From Earth, we find that galaxies are rushing away from us in every direction. They are not just rushing away from us, but also from one another. You can imagine the expansion by thinking of the universe as being like a balloon, with the galaxies scattered on the surface. With each extra blow into the balloon, the universe expands, and the galaxies move farther apart.

Galaxies were closer together in the early universe

Big Bang—origin of the universe's expansion

Distance between galaxies is increasing

Present-day universe

Universe a few billion years ago

THE EXPANDING UNIVERSE
In 1917, US astronomer Vesto Slipher found that most galaxies he studied were rushing away from us (see below). The universe seemed to be expanding. Using the Hooker telescope (above) at Mount Wilson Observatory, Edwin Hubble discovered that the rate of expansion depends on distance. The more distant a galaxy, the faster it is traveling.

Earth

Star moving away from Earth

Spectral lines formed by elements in star shift to the red

RED SHIFTS
When an ambulance speeds past us, we hear the pitch of its siren drop. The wavelength of sound waves reaching us is stretched as the source moves away and each wave takes longer to reach us. Similarly, light waves from a receding galaxy are stretched to longer (redder) wavelengths. The color change is hard to detect, but the shift is easily measured in changes to the dark "spectral lines."

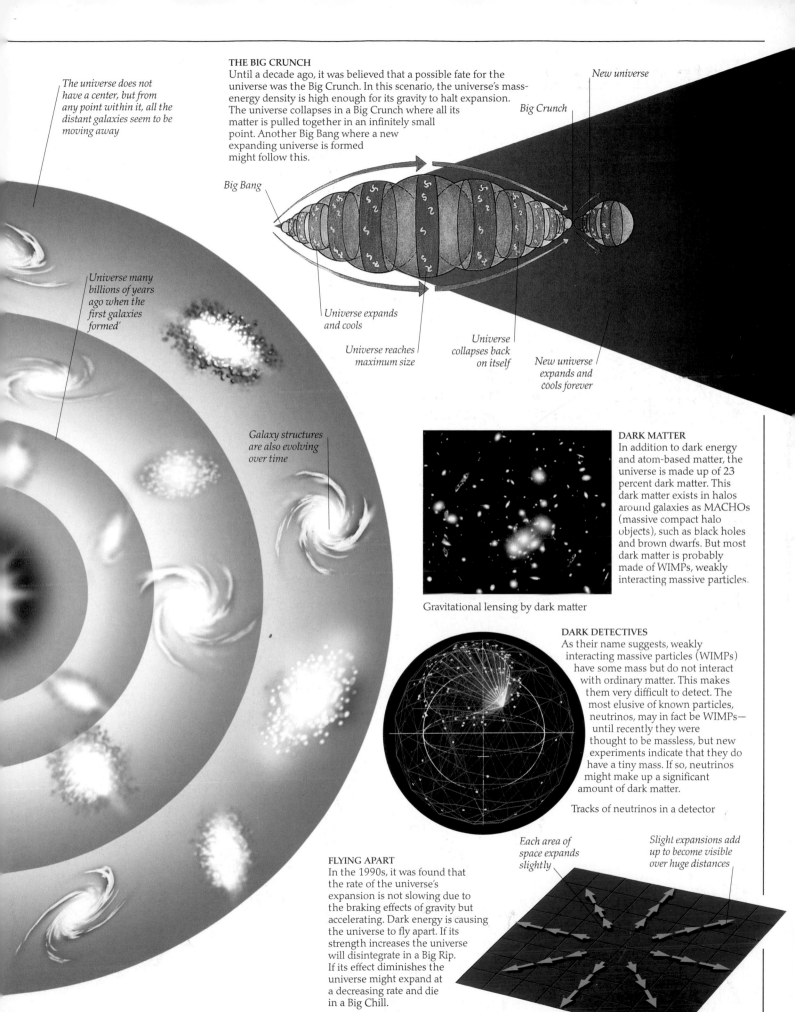

The universe does not have a center, but from any point within it, all the distant galaxies seem to be moving away

Universe many billions of years ago when the first galaxies formed'

Galaxy structures are also evolving over time

THE BIG CRUNCH

Until a decade ago, it was believed that a possible fate for the universe was the Big Crunch. In this scenario, the universe's mass-energy density is high enough for its gravity to halt expansion. The universe collapses in a Big Crunch where all its matter is pulled together in an infinitely small point. Another Big Bang where a new expanding universe is formed might follow this.

New universe

Big Crunch

Big Bang

Universe expands and cools

Universe reaches maximum size

Universe collapses back on itself

New universe expands and cools forever

DARK MATTER

In addition to dark energy and atom-based matter, the universe is made up of 23 percent dark matter. This dark matter exists in halos around galaxies as MACHOs (massive compact halo objects), such as black holes and brown dwarfs. But most dark matter is probably made of WIMPs, weakly interacting massive particles.

Gravitational lensing by dark matter

DARK DETECTIVES

As their name suggests, weakly interacting massive particles (WIMPs) have some mass but do not interact with ordinary matter. This makes them very difficult to detect. The most elusive of known particles, neutrinos, may in fact be WIMPs— until recently they were thought to be massless, but new experiments indicate that they do have a tiny mass. If so, neutrinos might make up a significant amount of dark matter.

Tracks of neutrinos in a detector

FLYING APART

In the 1990s, it was found that the rate of the universe's expansion is not slowing due to the braking effects of gravity but accelerating. Dark energy is causing the universe to fly apart. If its strength increases the universe will disintegrate in a Big Rip. If its effect diminishes the universe might expand at a decreasing rate and die in a Big Chill.

Each area of space expands slightly

Slight expansions add up to become visible over huge distances

Exploring the universe

ASTRONOMERS HAVE SPENT more than five millennia gazing at the heavens, studying the stars and constellations, following the Moon through its phases, watching the planets wander through the zodiac, seeing comets come and go, and witnessing eclipses. A giant leap in astronomy came when Galileo first turned a telescope on the heavens in 1609. Since then, ever larger telescopes have revealed ever more secrets of a universe vaster than anyone can imagine. Other kinds of telescopes have been built to study the invisible radiations stars and galaxies give out. Radio waves can be studied from the ground, but other rays have to be studied from space because Earth's atmosphere absorbs them as they pass through it.

LOOKING WITH LENSES
Some of the lens-type telescopes, or refractors, used by early astronomers reached an amazing size. They used small light-gathering lenses with a long "focal length" to achieve greater magnification. Christiaan Huygens' giant "aerial telescope" (above) was 210 ft (64 m) long.

Eyepiece

Incoming light rays

Aperture allows light to reach primary mirror

Magnetometer detects Earth's magnetic field

Light rays reflected inward

Primary mirror

Secondary mirror bounces light to eyepiece

NEWTONIAN REFLECTOR
Most astronomical telescopes use mirrors to gather and focus light. Some still follow Isaac Newton's original design of 1671. A large curved primary mirror gathers and focuses the light, reflecting it back along the telescope tube onto a secondary plane (flat) mirror. This mirror in turn reflects the light into an eyepiece mounted near the front of the tube. In most professional telescopes, the eyepiece is replaced by cameras or other instruments.

Mounting allows accurate pointing of telescope—this is a "Dobsonian" mount

THE HUBBLE SPACE TELESCOPE
The Hubble Space Telescope (HST) is a reflector with a 8-ft (2.4-m) diameter mirror. It circles Earth every 90 minutes in an orbit about 380 miles (610 km) high. It made a disastrous debut in 1990, when its primary mirror was found to be flawed. But its vision was corrected, and the satellite is now sending back some of the most spectacular images ever taken in space. High above the atmosphere, it views the universe with perfect clarity, not only at visible wavelengths but in the ultraviolet and infrared as well.

Solar arrays produce 3,000 watts of electricity

Comet Wild 2

GOING THERE
Space probes have been winging their way to explore the Moon, planets, and other bodies in the solar system since 1959. Some fly by their targets; some go into orbit around them; and others land. *Stardust* flew by Comet Wild 2 on January 2, 2004, and captured comet dust which it returned to Earth just over two years later.

Domes of the Keck Telescopes, Mauna Kea, Hawaii

Stardust probe

TWIN KECKS
The two Keck telescopes in Hawaii are among the most powerful in the world. They have light-gathering mirrors measuring 33 ft (10 m) across. These mirrors are made not in one piece, but from 36 separate segments. Each is individually supported and computer controlled so that it always forms, with the others, a perfect mirror shape. When the two telescopes are linked, they can create an effective mirror 280 ft (85 m) in diameter.

RADIO ASTRONOMY

The first radio signals from space were detected in 1931 by Bell Telephone engineer Karl Jansky. Because radio waves are so much longer than light waves, radio astronomers must use huge dishes to form a detailed image. Many radio astronomy observatories use sets of dishes in unison to form effective collecting areas miles across. The Very Large Array radio telescope near Socorro in New Mexico uses 27 dishes in various configurations. An even greater receiving area is produced by linking radio telescopes in different countries.

Telescopes of the Very Large Array

Sunshade prevents strong light from damaging instruments

Handrail for astronauts

High-gain antenna

Telescope tube is covered in insulating foil to prevent expansion and contraction as external temperature changes

HST is powered by two 22-ft (6.6-m) solar panels. Batteries store power for the dark periods of Hubble's orbit.

Housing for computers and other equipment

Position of primary mirror

Instrument segment houses cameras and spectrometers

Access panels allow individual instruments to be replaced and upgraded

Integral

High-gain antenna for communications with Earth. Pictures are sent back like TV signals

HIGH-ENERGY TELESCOPES

Telescopes like *Integral* are needed to detect high-energy radiation from the most violent regions of the universe—around quasars, supernovae, and black holes. Integral detects gamma rays; other telescopes such as XMM-Newton detect X-rays.

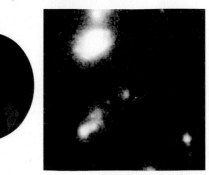

RECORD BREAKER

With its formidable resolution, the HST has been able to spot objects as far away as 13 billion light-years. Their light has taken so long to reach us that we are seeing them as they were when the universe was in its infancy.

HST image of a supernova 10 billion light-years away

Our corner of the universe

THE COPERNICAN SYSTEM
In 1543, Polish astronomer and priest Nicolaus Copernicus (1473–1543) put our corner of the universe in order, suggesting that the Sun and not Earth was at the center of our planetary system. The idea contradicted the teachings of the Church, but was eventually proved by Galileo.

ANCIENT ASTRONOMERS BELIEVED that Earth had to be the center of the universe. Didn't the Sun, the Moon, and all the other heavenly bodies and the stars revolve around it? Of course today we know they don't—the Sun is really the center of our little corner of the universe, and the Earth and planets circle around that body. They are part of the Sun's family, or solar system. The Sun is different from all other bodies in the solar system because it is a star, and it is the only body that produces light of its own. We see all the other objects by the sunlight they reflect. Eight planets, including Earth, are the most important members of the solar system, along with three dwarf planets and over one hundred and fifty moons. The billions of minor members include rocky lumps called asteroids and icy bodies called comets.

PLANETS
A planet is a world massive enough to pull itself into a roughly spherical shape that orbits the Sun in a neighborhood cleared of other objects. Our planet Earth is the third from the Sun, and its position provides perfect conditions for life.

MOONS
All the planets except Mercury and Venus have satellites, or moons, circling around them. The four giant outer planets have more than 150 moons between them. This is Saturn's moon Mimas.

Mercury

Neptune takes 164.8 years to orbit the Sun

Mars takes 1.9 years to orbit the Sun

Mars

Pluto

Pluto takes 248 years to orbit the Sun once; it was classed as a planet from its discovery in 1930 until 2006

Jupiter takes 11.9 years to orbit the Sun

Uranus

Jupiter

Asteroid Belt contains the dwarf planet Ceres and billions of asteroids

Saturn takes 29.5 years to orbit the Sun

Uranus takes 84 years to orbit the Sun

DWARF PLANETS IN KUIPER BELT
Beyond Neptune is the Kuiper Belt of rock-and-ice objects. The largest are the dwarf planets Eris (above) and Pluto. Dwarf planets are a class of almost round bodies orbiting the Sun, introduced in 2006. Since 2008 they are also known as plutoids—dwarf planets in the Kuiper Belt.

Gas and dust collapse into disk

Central regions heat up

HOW IT ALL BEGAN

Five billion years ago there was nothing in our corner of space but a huge billowing cloud of gas and dust, which had remained unchanged for millions of years. Then something disturbed it, and it began to collapse and spin under gravity. Over time, a thick disk of matter formed, which had a denser region at the center. This central mass became progressively denser and hotter and evolved into our Sun. Once the Sun had formed, the surrounding disk thinned out and formed into separate planets.

Sun ignites and blows away much of surrounding gas cloud

Planets formed as at first tiny and then increasingly large particles came together

Asteroid Ida

ASTEROIDS

Sometimes called minor planets, the asteroids are lumps of rock and sometimes metal left over from the formation of the solar system. They are found mainly in the space between the orbits of Mars and Jupiter, in a region known as the Asteroid Belt. However, some asteroids stray outside the Asteroid Belt and may come uncomfortably close to Earth. The space probe *Galileo* photographed asteroid Ida on its way to Jupiter in 1995—it is about 35 miles (55 km) long.

All eight planets follow orbits close to the plane of the Sun's equator, which is called the plane of the ecliptic

"We shall prove Earth to be a wandering body... and not the sink of all dull refuse of the universe."

GALILEO

Near Earth Asteroids orbit close to our planet

Sun

Venus

Earth

Neptune

Saturn

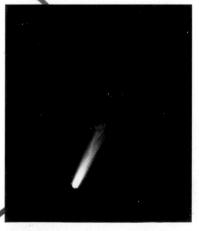

Some asteroids, called Trojans, share Jupiter's orbit

MAP OF THE SOLAR SYSTEM

The planets orbit the Sun at different distances, from about 36 million miles (58 million km) for innermost Mercury, to about 2.8 billion miles (4.5 billion km) for the outermost planet Neptune. The planets don't move in perfect circles but in elliptical (oval) orbits, trapped by the pull of the Sun's gravity. They travel in much the same plane.

COMETS

Comets are icy bodies that form a vast sphere called the Oort Cloud, which surrounds the planetary part of the solar system. Occasionally one leaves the cloud and travels in toward the Sun. The heat turns its snow and ice to gas and the comet becomes big and bright enough to be seen.

Our local star

THE STAR WE CALL THE SUN dominates our corner of space. With a diameter of about 870,000 miles (1,400,000 km), it is more than a hundred times wider than Earth. Because of its huge mass, it has powerful gravity and attracts a vast collection of objects both large (such as Earth and the other planets) and small (such as comets). These bodies form the Sun's family, or solar system. Like other stars, the Sun is a great ball of incandescent gas, or rather, gases. The two main ones are hydrogen and helium, but there are small amounts of more than 70 other chemical elements as well. To us on Earth, 93 million miles (150 million kilometers) away, the Sun is all-important. It provides the light and warmth needed to make our planet suitable for life.

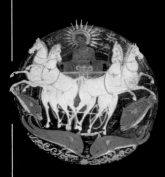

SUN LEGENDS
The Sun was worshiped as a god from the earliest times. In ancient Egypt, the falcon-headed Sun god Re was the most powerful deity. In early Greek mythology, the Sun god Helios carried the Sun across the heavens every day in a horse-drawn flying chariot.

Visible surface of the Sun is called the photosphere

Prominences are fountains of hot gas that loop above the surface

The Sun's visible surface is made up of fine "granulations"

Photosphere's temperature is around 9,900°F (5,500°C)

Corona extends millions of miles into space

THE SOLAR CYCLE
The Sun has powerful magnetism, which gives rise to sunspots, prominences, and huge outbursts called flares. Magnetism and activity vary regularly over a period of about 11 years. This is called the solar, or sunspot cycle. Over this period, activity on the Sun goes from minimum to maximum and back again, as shown in this series of X-ray images.

X-rays from hot magnetized gas

Sun emits most X-rays at maximum

Moon blots out Sun's surface during total eclipse

Convective zone

Radiative zone

SUNSPOTS
Sunspots are dark patches on the Sun's surface, about 2,700°F (1,500°C) cooler than the surrounding surface. They vary from short-lived "pores" less than 600 miles (1,000 km) across to huge features a hundred times bigger that persist for months.

Photosphere at about 9,900°F (5,500°C)

THE CORONA
An extensive atmosphere of gases surrounds the Sun, gradually thinning until it merges into space. We can see the pearly white outer atmosphere, or corona ("crown"), only during a total eclipse, when the Sun's brilliant surface is blotted out. Temperatures in the corona can hit 5.4 million°F (3 million°C).

INSIDE THE SUN
The Sun is a great ball of glowing gas that is hottest and most dense at the center, or core. There, in a kind of nuclear furnace, fusion reactions produce the energy that keeps the Sun shining. Energy takes over a million years to transfer from the core to the surface—first by radiation, then by convection, or currents of rising gas.

Core, temperature about 27 million°F (15 million°C)

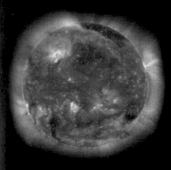

HIGH-ENERGY SUN
The Sun radiates not only light and heat, but also ultraviolet rays and X-rays. These forms of radiation pack great energy and pose a danger to life on Earth. Fortunately, our planet's atmosphere prevents most of the ultraviolet and all the X-rays from reaching the ground.

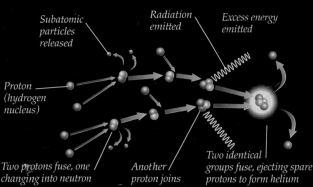

Subatomic particles released

Radiation emitted

Excess energy emitted

Proton (hydrogen nucleus)

Two protons fuse, one changing into neutron

Another proton joins

Two identical groups fuse, ejecting spare protons to form helium

The nuclear fusion process

THE SOLAR FURNACE
Within the Sun's core, energy is produced by nuclear fusion reactions. In fusion, four hydrogen atom nuclei (centers) join together or fuse to form the nucleus of a helium atom—a process that can only happen at tremendous temperatures and pressures. In the process, a tiny amount of excess mass is lost, transformed directly into a vast amount of energy.

Earth's Moon

Bright crater surrounded by rays

THE MOON IS EARTH'S CLOSEST companion in space, its only natural satellite. On average, it lies 239,000 miles (384,000 km) away. It has no light of its own, but shines by reflected sunlight. As the Moon circles the Earth every month, it appears to change shape, from slim crescent to full circle, and back again every 29.5 days. We call these changing shapes the phases of the Moon, and they mark one of the great rhythms of nature. With a diameter of 2,160 miles (3,476 km), the Moon is a rocky world like Earth, but has no atmosphere, water, or life. Astronomers think that the Moon was formed from the debris flung into space in a collision between Earth and a Mars-sized body about 4.5 billion years ago.

New Moon

Crescent

First quarter

Waxing gibbous

Full Moon

Waning gibbous

Last quarter

The dark part of the crescent Moon sometimes dimly reflects light from Earth

Decrescent

Actor Lon Chaney Jr. in The *Wolf Man* (1941)

LUNAR LEGENDS
The Greeks and Romans worshiped the Moon as the goddess Artemis or Diana. Ancient people thought the Moon had magic powers, and that staying too long in the light of the full Moon could make them insane. Our word lunatic comes from *luna*, the Latin word for the Moon. People also believed the full Moon could turn some people into werewolves who preyed on humans and ate human flesh.

Craters formed when meteorites crashed into the Moon

THE CHANGING FACE
The changing phases of the Moon happen as the Sun lights up different amounts of the side that faces Earth. At new Moon we can't see the Moon at all because the Sun is lighting up only the far side. As the Moon moves farther around in its orbit, more and more of its face gets lit up until all of it is illuminated at full Moon. Then the sunlit side moves on and the Moon's phase decreases, until it disappears completely.

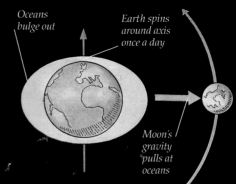

Oceans bulge out

Earth spins around axis once a day

Moon's gravity pulls at oceans

LUNAR GRAVITY
The Moon's gravity is only about one-sixth of Earth's, so it has been unable to hang onto any gases to make an atmosphere. The lack of atmosphere means the temperature varies widely from day (around 230°F, 110°C) to night (around -290°F, -180°C). Weak though it is, the Moon's gravity still affects Earth. It tugs at the oceans to create tides. The water bulges to form a high tide directly beneath the Moon and also forms a bulge on the opposite side of Earth. On either side of high tide is a low tide where water has been drawn away. There are two highs and two lows roughly every day.

THE FACE OF THE MOON

The Moon always presents the same face toward Earth. This happens because it spins once on its axis in exactly the same time as it circles once around Earth—27.3 days. This motion is called captured rotation and other large moons do it. The dark regions we see on the Moon's face are vast dusty plains. Early astronomers thought they might be seas and called them *maria*, which is Latin for seas. The brighter regions are much older highlands, which are heavily cratered and are thought to be part of the Moon's original crust.

Aitken Basin is the largest crater in the solar system

The Moon's south polar region

WALKING ON THE MOON

On July 20, 1969, *Apollo 11* astronauts Neil Armstrong and Buzz Aldrin planted the first human footprints on the Moon. They were the first of 12 US astronauts who explored "seas" and highland areas, set up scientific stations, and brought back samples of soil and rock. They found that lunar soil, called regolith, is somewhat like plowed-up soil on Earth—it has been crushed by constant bombardment from space. The majority of the rocks are volcanic, often like Earth rocks called basalts.

THE HIDDEN POLES

We never see the Moon's poles from Earth, but space probes have inspected them. They show that some polar craters and basins are in perpetual darkness and could contain hidden deposits of ice. If proven, these ice deposits could provide water for future human explorers.

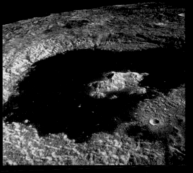

THE FAR SIDE

No one had seen the far side of the Moon until orbiting probes mapped it in the 1960s. It is much more rugged and heavily cratered than the nearside and has no large "seas." One of its most prominent features is the 115-mile (185-km) crater Tsiolkovsky.

Dark maria (seas) are plains of solidified lava

Lunar highlands

Seen from the Moon, the Earth goes through phases

Lunar surface many miles below

EARTHRISE

The *Apollo* astronauts took stunning photographs of the Moon on the surface and also from orbit. None are more dramatic than the shots showing Earth rising over the Moon's horizon. They show the huge contrast between our colorful, living world and its drab, dead satellite.

Comparing the planets

GOING OUT FROM THE SUN, the eight planets are
Mercury, Venus, Earth, Mars, Jupiter, Saturn, Uranus,
and Neptune. They are all different from one another,
but divide mainly into two kinds, depending on their
composition. The four small inner planets are made up
mainly of rock, and the four giant outer ones are made
up mainly of gas. All the planets have two motions in
space: the period in which a planet spins on its axis
is its rotation period, sometimes thought of as
its "day," and the time it takes to make one
orbit of the Sun is its "year."

THE PLANETS TO SCALE
The planets vary widely in size. Jupiter is truly
gigantic, containing more matter than all the other
planets put together. It could swallow more than
1,300 bodies the size of the Earth and over 25,000
worlds the size of Mercury. Yet the cores at the
centers of the giant planets are much smaller—
around the size of Earth. At the other extreme,
Mercury is tiny—Jupiter and Saturn each have
a moon bigger than Mercury.

MERCURY
*Diameter: 3,032 miles/
4,880 km
Distance from Sun:
36 million miles/
58 million km
Rotation period: 58.7 days
Time to orbit Sun: 88 days
No. of moons: 0*

EARTH
*Diameter: 7,926 miles/12,756 km
Distance from Sun:
93 million miles/
149.6 million km
Rotation period: 23.93 hours
Time to orbit Sun: 365.25 days
No. of moons: 1*

VENUS
*Diameter: 7,521 miles/
12,104 km
Distance from Sun:
67 million miles/108 million km
Rotation period: 243 days
Time to orbit Sun: 224.7 days
No. of moons: 0*

MARS
*Diameter: 4,222 miles/
6,794 km
Distance from Sun:
142 million miles/
228 million km
Rotation period: 24.6 hours
Time to orbit Sun: 687 days
No. of moons: 2*

*Most gas giants have
turbulent atmospheres
powered by an internal
energy source*

JUPITER
*Diameter: 88,846 miles/142,984 km
Distance from Sun: 484 million miles/
778 million km
Rotation period: 9.93 hours
Time to orbit Sun: 11.9 years
No. of moons: 63*

ORBITS TO SCALE
The diagram across the bottom of this page
shows the distances of the planets from the
Sun to scale. The four inner planets lie
relatively close together, while the four outer
planets lie very far apart. The solar system
consists mainly of empty space.

*An extensive system of rings surrounds
Saturn's equator, spanning a distance of
over 250,000 miles (400,000 km) out
from the edge of the planet. All four gas
giants have ring systems, but Saturn's
rings are by far the most impressive.*

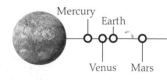

Mercury
Earth
Venus Mars
Jupiter
Saturn

IN THE ECLIPTIC

The planets circle the Sun close to a flat plane called the plane of the ecliptic. In Earth's skies, the ecliptic is the path the Sun appears to take through the heavens during a year. From Earth, the planets appear to travel close to this plane, through the constellations of the zodiac. Dust around the ecliptic causes a faint glow in the night sky called the zodiacal light.

The five naked-eye planets aligned along the ecliptic

SATURN
Diameter: 74,900 miles/120,536 km
Distance from Sun:
887 million miles/1,429 million km
Rotation period: 10.66 hours
Time to orbit Sun: 29.5 years
No. of moons: 60

As shown by the tilt of Saturn's rings, planets do not orbit the Sun bolt upright—most are tilted over to some extent

URANUS
Diameter: 31,770 miles
/51,118 km
Distance from Sun:
1.79 billion miles/
2,875 million km
Rotation period: 17.24 hours
Time to orbit Sun: 84 years
No. of moons: 27

NEPTUNE
Diameter: 30,780 miles/49,532 km
Distance from Sun: 2.8 billion miles
/4,505 million km
Rotation period: 16.11 hours
Time to or bit Sun: 164.8 years
No. of moons: 13

GAS GIANTS

The four planets from Jupiter to Neptune are gas giants. They have a deep atmosphere of mainly hydrogen and helium. Underneath the atmosphere is a planet-wide ocean of liquid hydrogen in Jupiter and Saturn, or of slushy ices in the smaller giants. Only at the center is there a small core of rock. The gas giants have two other things in common: they have many moons circling around them, and they have systems of rings.

Outer atmosphere

Liquid hydrogen molecules

Structure of Jupiter

Liquid atomic hydrogen

Core

ROCKY PLANETS

The four inner planets, from Mercury to Mars, have a similar, rocky structure. They are known as the terrestrial or Earthlike planets. They have a thin, hard outer layer, or crust, which overlays another thicker layer called the mantle. In the center is a core of metal, mainly iron. All the planets except Mercury have an atmosphere.

Mantle

Core

Crust

Atmosphere

Structure of Mars

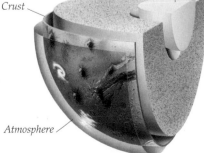

Uranus

Neptune

Mercury and Venus

Crust

Mantle

Core

TWO ROCKY PLANETS, Mercury and Venus, orbit closer to the Sun than Earth. We see them shining in the night sky like bright stars. Venus is by far the brightest, shining prominently for much of the year as the evening star. Mercury lies so close to the Sun that it is only visible briefly at certain times of year, just before sunrise or just after sunset. Both planets are much hotter than Earth—surface temperatures on Mercury can rise as high as 840°F (450°C), and on Venus up to 55°F (30°C) higher. But the two planets are very different. Mercury is less than half as big across as Venus, is almost completely covered in craters, and has no appreciable atmosphere. Venus has a very dense atmosphere, full of clouds, which stops us seeing the surface underneath.

INSIDE MERCURY

Mercury is a small planet, with a diameter of 3,032 miles (4,880 km). It is rocky like Earth and has a similar layered structure. Underneath a hard outer layer, or crust, it has a rocky mantle, then a core of iron. The core is unusually large, extending three-quarters of the way to the surface.

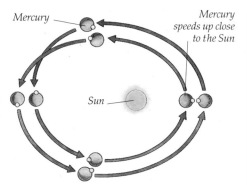

Mercury

Mercury speeds up close to the Sun

Sun

SPEEDY ORBIT

Mercury is the fastest-moving planet, orbiting the Sun in just 88 days. But it rotates very slowly, just once in roughly 59 days. As a result, Mercury rotates three times every two orbits (shown by the dot in the diagram) and there is an interval of 176 Earth days between one sunrise and the next. Temperatures vary from 840°F (450°C) in daytime to -290°F (-180°C) at night.

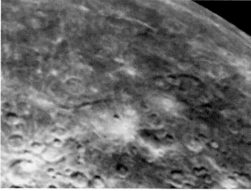

THE CRATERED SURFACE

Mercury was heavily bombarded with meteorites billions of years ago, resulting in the heavily cratered, Moonlike landscape we see today. There are some smoother plains here and there, but nothing like the Moon's seas. The biggest feature is the huge Caloris Basin, an impact crater about 800 miles (1,300 km) across.

Clouds of sulfuric acid

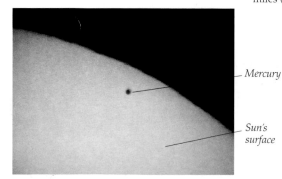

Mercury

Sun's surface

TRANSITS

Mercury and Venus circle the Sun inside Earth's orbit and can sometimes pass in front of the Sun as seen from Earth. We call these crossings transits. They are rare because Earth, the planets, and the Sun only very occasionally line up precisely in space. Transits of Venus are rarest, coming in pairs every century or so.

COOK'S TOUR

In 1768, Britain's Royal Society appointed James Cook to command the first scientific expedition to the Pacific Ocean. One of the expedition's prime goals was to record the transit of Venus from Tahiti on June 3, 1769, which could be used to measure the distance from Earth to the Sun. After making these measurements, Cook sailed his ship *Endeavour* to New Zealand and Australia, where in 1770 he landed at Botany Bay. He claimed the land for Britain and named it New South Wales.

Earth's deadly twin

Venus and Earth are almost identical in size but are very different worlds. At 7,521 miles (12,104 km) across, Venus is the smaller of the two. Its very high temperature and crushing atmosphere make it a most hostile planet, and its clouds are made up of droplets of sulfuric acid. If you went to Venus, you would simultaneously be burned, crushed, and roasted to death—and suffocated, too, because the atmosphere is nearly all carbon dioxide.

Solar panels

Magellan *radar map of volcanoes on Venus*

Surface of Venus below the clouds

Radar antenna

Magellan Venus probe

VOLCANIC WORLD

Venus's surface has been shaped by volcanoes and some are possibly still active. Wave upon wave of lava flows can be seen where the volcanoes have erupted. Other geological activity has also created strange structures—circular coronae and spidery networks called arachnoids. Volcanic eruptions have also wiped out most traces of impact craters on Venus.

THROUGH THE CLOUDS

We can't actually see the surface of Venus because of the clouds, but we can use radar to image the surface, because radio waves can penetrate the cloud cover. Orbiting space probes like *Magellan* (1990–1994) have now mapped virtually all of Venus, revealing a mostly low-lying planet with just a few highland regions. The largest are two continentlike outcrops, Ishtar Terra in the north and Aphrodite Terra near the equator.

GODDESS OF LOVE

Venus is named after the Roman goddess of love and beauty; the Greeks called her Aphrodite. This female theme is reflected in the names given to Venus's features. The continent Ishtar Terra is named after the Babylonian goddess of love. There is a crater called Cleopatra, a plain called Guinevere, and a deep valley (chasma) called Diana.

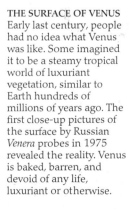

Venus de Milo in the Louvre, Paris

Atmosphere is transparent beneath the clouds

19th-century artist's impression

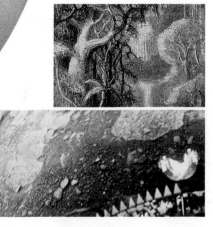

1982 *Venera* photograph of Venus's surface

THE SURFACE OF VENUS

Early last century, people had no idea what Venus was like. Some imagined it to be a steamy tropical world of luxuriant vegetation, similar to Earth hundreds of millions of years ago. The first close-up pictures of the surface by Russian *Venera* probes in 1975 revealed the reality. Venus is baked, barren, and devoid of any life, luxuriant or otherwise.

Home planet

WITH A DIAMETER of 7,926 miles (12,756 km) at the equator, Earth is Venus's near twin in size, but the similarity ends there. At an average distance of 93 million miles (150 million km) from the Sun, Earth is not a hellish place like Venus, but a comfortable world that is a haven for all kinds of life. It is a rocky planet like the other three inner planets of the solar system, but is the only one whose surface is not solid—instead, it is broken up into a number of sections, called plates. The plates move slowly over the surface, causing the continents to drift and the oceans to widen.

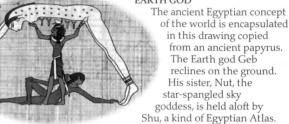

EARTH GOD
The ancient Egyptian concept of the world is encapsulated in this drawing copied from an ancient papyrus. The Earth god Geb reclines on the ground. His sister, Nut, the star-spangled sky goddess, is held aloft by Shu, a kind of Egyptian Atlas.

Temperate regions between poles and equator experience a moderate, changing climate

Earth's oceans are on average over 2.5 miles (4 km) deep

PLATE TECTONICS
The study of Earth's shifting crust is known as plate tectonics. At plate boundaries, colliding plates may destroy rocks and create volcanoes. Here, at the San Andreas fault in California, plates grind past each other and cause earthquakes.

INSIDE EARTH
Earth has a layered structure, a bit like an onion. It has an outer layer, or crust, of hard rock. This is very thin, averaging about 25 miles (40 km) on the continents but only about 6 miles (10 km) under the oceans. The crust overlays a heavier rocky mantle, the top part of which is relatively soft and can flow. Deeper down lies a huge iron core. The outer core is liquid, while the inner core is solid. Currents and eddies in the liquid outer core are believed to give rise to Earth's magnetism.

OCEANS AND ATMOSPHERE
Oceans cover more than 70 percent of Earth's surface. The evaporation of ocean water into the atmosphere plays a crucial role in the planet's climate. This never-ending exchange of moisture between the surface and atmosphere dictates weather patterns around the globe. Most of Earth's weather takes place in the troposphere, the lowest layer of atmosphere, up to about 10 miles (16 km) high.

Earth seen from orbit

Ice caps cover North and South poles

Crust of silicate minerals floats on molten interior

Arid desert regions lie close to the equator

Earth bulges at the equator—its diameter here is 13 miles (21 km) more than at the poles

Antarctica

Death Valley, California

CLIMATE EXTREMES
Antarctica experiences the coldest temperatures on Earth, with a low of -128.6°F (-89.2°C) recorded at Vostok Station in 1983. Death Valley in California is one of the world's hottest places, where temperatures regularly nudge 122°F (50°C) in summer.

Inner core of solid iron

Outer core of molten iron and nickel

Core may contain a small dense "kernel" at its very center

THE MAGNETIC SHIELD
Earth's magnetism extends into space, creating a bubblelike cocoon around our planet called the magnetosphere. It acts as a shield against deadly radiation and particles streaming out from the Sun. However, particles trapped in the magnetosphere are often shaken out over the poles. As they interact with the upper atmosphere, they create the beautiful light displays we call the aurorae, or northern and southern lights.

Aurorae photographed from the Space Shuttle

Outer mantle

Inner mantle richer in iron than outer mantle

Although shown upright, Earth's poles are in fact tilted 23.5° from vertical. As Earth orbits the Sun, one pole and then the other gets more sunlight, creating the seasons.

LIFE IN ABUNDANCE
With comfortable temperatures, liquid water, and oxygen in the atmosphere, Earth can support an amazing variety of life. This can vary from primitive microscopic organisms like viruses and bacteria to towering redwood trees and a multitude of flowering plants; from creepy-crawly creatures like slugs and spiders to warm-blooded birds and intelligent mammals, like ourselves.

Life thriving on and around a coral reef

Mars, the Red Planet

THE REDDISH HUE OF MARS makes it a distinctive member of our solar system. Mars was named after the Roman god of war. With a diameter of 4,222 miles (6,794 km), Mars is about half the size of Earth, but it is like our planet in several respects. Its day is only about half an hour longer than our own. It also has seasons, an atmosphere, and ice caps at the poles. But in other ways, Mars is very different. Its atmosphere is very thin and contains mainly carbon dioxide. The surface is barren and the average temperature is below freezing. Conditions now are not suitable for life, but recent findings support the theory that Mars was once a warmer, wetter place.

Northern half of Mars is mostly low-lying plains

Valles Marineris canyon system is 4 miles (6 km) deep in places

Southern hemisphere is dominated by Moonlike, cratered highlands

A WET WORLD?
We have known for years that Mars has water ice in its polar caps, but recent observations by the Mars Odyssey spacecraft suggest that ice is present in the soil as well, particularly in southern polar regions. On this map the icy regions are colored deep blue. In these areas, as much as 50 percent of the top 3 ft (1 m) of soil could be water ice.

EXPLORING THE SURFACE

The surface of Mars has been more extensively explored than that of any planet other than Earth. Craft such as *Mars Express* (since 2003) have photographed its landscape from orbit and landing probes such as the two *Vikings* (1976) and *Mars Pathfinder* (1997) have taken close-up pictures of its surface. These pictures show rust-colored rocks strewn across a sandy surface. *Mars Pathfinder* released the *Sojourner* rover that explored an ancient floodplain. Twin rovers *Spirit* and *Opportunity* have been exploring the surface since January 2004. Each is a robot geologist using its cameras and tools to locate signs of past water activity on Mars.

Phobos

Deimos

DOGS OF WAR

Mars has two moons, Phobos and Deimos (meaning Fear and Terror). Both are tiny—Phobos measures about 16 miles (26 km) across; Deimos, just 10 miles (16 km). Astronomers think they are asteroids that Mars captured long ago. They are dark and rich in carbon, like many asteroids.

Rockstrewn landscape of Ares Vallis region

Sojourner rover

ON TOP OF THE WORLD

Olympus Mons (Mount Olympus) is the largest of four big volcanoes near Mars's equator. It rises some 15 miles (24 km) above its surroundings—nearly three times higher than Mount Everest. Measuring 370 miles (600 km) across its base, it has a summit caldera (crater) 56 miles (90 km) wide. It probably last erupted about 25 million years ago.

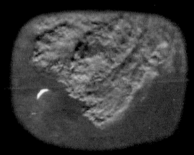

MARTIAN WEATHER

Although Mars has only a slight atmosphere, strong winds often blow across the surface, reaching speeds as high as 200 mph (300 kph). They whip up fine particles from the surface to create dust storms that can sometimes shroud the whole planet.

Deadly heat ray

Martian war machine

THE MARTIANS ARE COMING

Thoughts of a desperate Martian race, fighting to survive in an increasingly hostile climate, stimulated the imaginations of many people, including English author H. G. Wells. In 1898, he published a groundbreaking science fiction novel entitled *The War of the Worlds*. It featured a Martian invasion of Earth, with terrifying, invincible war machines and weapons. A masterly radio adaptation of the invasion by Orson Welles, presented as though it were a news report, created a minor panic in the United States in 1938.

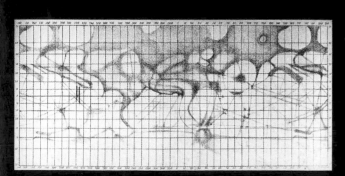

THE CANALS OF MARS

Italian astronomer Giovanni Schiaparelli first reported seeing *canali* (channels) on Mars in 1877. This led other astronomers to suppose that there was a dying Martian race digging canals to irrigate parched farmland. Prominent among them was Percival Lowell, who produced maps of the canal systems.

1907 illustration from *The War of the Worlds*

Jupiter, king of the planets

Jupiter is 88,846 miles (142,984 km) in diameter

MORE MASSIVE THAN ALL THE OTHER PLANETS put together, Jupiter is the largest member of the solar system after the Sun. The planet is one of the gas giants, with an atmosphere of hydrogen and helium above a vast ocean of liquid hydrogen. Its colorful face is crossed by dark and pale bands, called belts and zones. These are clouds that have been drawn out by the planet's rapid rotation—Jupiter spins around once in less than 10 hours. This high-speed spin also causes the planet to bulge noticeably around its equator. At least 63 moons circle the planet, but only the four so-called Galilean moons are large. Jupiter also has a ring system around it, but it is small and much too faint to be seen from Earth.

RULER OF THE GODS
Jupiter is an appropriate name for the king of the planets, because Jupiter was the king of the gods in Roman mythology. The ancient Greeks called him Zeus, and told stories of his many amorous conquests. All Jupiter's moons except one (Amalthea) are named after Zeus's lovers and descendants.

Antenna sends data back to Earth and receives instructions

Heat from nuclear fuel powers the spacecraft

Science instruments

GALILEO TO JUPITER
The US space probe *Galileo* went into orbit around Jupiter in 1995 after a five-year journey through space, using gravity boosts from Venus and Earth. *Galileo* confirmed that the top layer of Jupiter's clouds consists of ammonia ice; it detected winds in the atmosphere speeding at 400 mph (650 kph); and data collected from Europa suggest the moon may have a liquid ocean beneath its surface ice.

Earth to same scale

GREAT RED SPOT
Jupiter's Great Red Spot has been seen for more than 300 years. It seems to be a super-hurricane, with winds swirling around counterclockwise at high speeds. The Spot towers 5 miles (8 km) above the surrounding cloud tops as the swirling currents rise. It changes in size, but averages about 25,000 miles (40,000 km) across. Its vivid red color is probably due to the presence of phosphorus or perhaps carbon compounds.

TARGET JUPITER
In July 1994, the 20 or so fragments of Comet Shoemaker-Levy 9 smashed into Jupiter after the giant planet had disrupted the comet's orbit. The impacts created huge fireballs in the atmosphere up to 2,500 miles (4,000 km) across. The "scars" persisted for weeks.

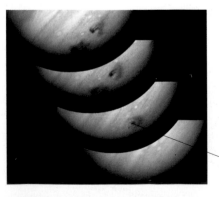

The plume (bottom) and the developing scar made by the impact of a comet fragment

IO

The most colorful moon in the solar system, Io is covered with flows of sulfur from many volcanoes. Volcanic eruptions send plumes of sulfur dioxide gas shooting 150 miles (250 km) above the surface. With a diameter of 2,264 miles (3,643 km), Io is about the same size as the Moon.

Sulfur-covered surface

Volcanic eruption on Io

EUROPA

Europa's surface reflects light well

Europa, diameter 1,945 miles (3,130 km), has a relatively smooth icy surface. A network of grooves and ridges crisscrosses the surface, showing where the icy crust has cracked. Some astronomers think that a liquid ocean could lie beneath the ice and might be a haven for life. Both Europa and Io are heated up by the gravitational tug of Jupiter.

Cracks in Europa's surface ice

GANYMEDE

Light areas seem to show where ice has welled up from inside Ganymede

Ganymede, diameter 3,273 miles (5,268 km), is not only Jupiter's biggest moon, but also the biggest in the whole solar system. It is bigger even than the planet Mercury. Ganymede has an old icy surface, with dark areas and paler grooved regions. Craters are widespread, with recent ones showing up white, where fresh ice has been exposed. Astronomers believe that Ganymede probably has a core of molten iron, like Earth.

Dark regions of older surface

CALLISTO

Callisto orbits farther out than Ganymede and is a little smaller (diameter 2,986 miles/4,806 km). It looks quite different, being almost completely covered with craters. Its crust is thought to be very ancient, dating back billions of years. From variations detected in the moon's magnetism, astronomers think that there might be a salty ocean underneath its icy crust.

Dark surface

Bright craters reveal fresh ice below surface

GALILEO'S MOONS

Italian astronomer Galileo Galilei was among the first to observe the heavens through a telescope (above) in 1609. He saw mountains on the Moon, sunspots, and Venus's phases. He also saw the four biggest moons of Jupiter, which are now known as the Galilean moons.

Saturn, the ringed wonder

SATURN IS EVERYONE'S FAVORITE PLANET because of the glorious system of shining rings that girdles its equator. Three other planets have rings—Jupiter, Uranus, and Neptune—but they are no rival to Saturn's. In the solar system, Saturn is the sixth planet from the Sun, orbiting at an average distance of about 888 million miles (1.4 billion km). The second largest planet after Jupiter, it measures 74,900 miles (120,536 km) across at the equator. Saturn is made up mainly of hydrogen and helium around a rocky core, like Jupiter, but is even less dense. Indeed, Saturn is so light that it would float in water. In appearance, the planet's surface is a pale imitation of Jupiter's, with faint bands of clouds drawn out by its rapid rotation.

THE RING CYCLE
Saturn's axis is tilted in space at an angle of nearly 27 degrees. Because of this, we see the ring system at various angles during the planet's journey around the Sun. Twice during the near-30-year orbit, the rings lie edge-on to Earth, and almost disappear from view.

B ring

Shadow cast by Saturn across rings

F ring

Shadow of rings on planet

INSIDE THE RINGS
Pictures taken by the *Voyager* probes show that Saturn's rings are made up of thousands of narrow ringlets. The ringlets are formed from chunks of matter whizzing around in orbit at high speed. These chunks are made of dirty water ice and vary widely in size from particles the size of sand grains to lumps as big as boulders.

RING WORLD
Through telescopes, astronomers can make out three rings around Saturn—working inward these are the A, B, and C rings. The broadest and brightest ring is the B ring, while the faintest is the C ring (also called the Crepe ring). The B ring is separated from the A ring by the Cassini Division, and there is a smaller gap, called the Encke Division, near the edge of the A ring. The space probes *Pioneer 11* and *Voyagers 1* and *2* discovered several other rings—a very faint D ring extends from the C ring nearly down to Saturn's cloud tops, and F, G, and E rings lie beyond the A ring. Overall, the ring system extends out from the planet about three and a half times Saturn's diameter.

MYSTERY PLANET
Early astronomers were puzzled by Saturn's strange appearance. In his book *Systema Saturnium* (1659), Dutch astronomer Christiaan Huygens showed drawings of Saturn by astronomers from Galileo (I) onward and examined various explanations of its unusual appearance. Huygens concluded that the planet was, in fact, surrounded by a thin, flat ring.

GIOVANNI CASSINI
Late 17th-century astronomers believed that Saturn's rings must be solid or liquid. But doubts emerged in 1675, when Italian astronomer Giovanni Domenico Cassini (1625–1712) discovered a dark line in Saturn's ring. This proved to be a gap between two rings, and became known as the Cassini Division. Cassini realized then that the rings couldn't be solid, but their true structure was not resolved until the 19th century.

Saturn's rapid rotation makes it bulge out at the equator

STORM WORLD
The bands in Saturn's atmosphere are streams of gases coursing around the planet at high speeds and in opposite directions. At the boundary between streams, the atmosphere gets churned up and furious storms break out. This false-color picture highlights three such regions.

SNOW WHITE
With a diameter of about 300 miles (500 km), Enceladus is the sixth largest of Saturn's 60 moons and by far the brightest. Parts of its icy surface are cratered and crisscrossed with grooves, but much of it is very smooth and is geologically much younger.

B ring

Cassini division

D ring

C ring

Inner A ring

Encke division

Outer A ring

Thick orange clouds block our view of Titan's surface

PLANET-SIZED TITAN
Saturn's largest moon, Titan, is huge. With a diameter of 3,200 miles (5,150 km), it is bigger than Mercury and second only to Ganymede among the solar system's moons. It is also unique because it is covered with a thick atmosphere that we can only see through in long wavelengths such as infrared waves.

Infrared map of Titan's surface

UNDER THE CLOUDS
Titan's atmosphere is mainly hydrogen, with traces of other gases, including methane. In 2005, the *Huygens* space probe descended through the atmosphere to Titan's surface. It recorded river- and channel-like features, and in July 2006 lakes of liquid methane were imaged by the *Cassini* probe (upper right) as it passed overhead.

New worlds

FOR CENTURIES, NO ONE seriously thought there might be planets too faint to see with the naked eye, lying in the darkness beyond Saturn. But in March 1781, musician-turned-astronomer William Herschel discovered one. Later named Uranus, this seventh planet proved to orbit the Sun at a distance of 1,79 billion miles (2,88 billion km), twice as far away as Saturn. At a stroke, Herschel's discovery had doubled the size of the known solar system! Oddities in Uranus's orbit suggested that another planet's gravity might be at work. This planet, Neptune, was eventually discovered by Johann Galle. Much later, in 1930, Clyde Tombaugh discovered Pluto, which was thought of as a ninth planet until 2006.

A WORLD ON EDGE
Uranus is the third largest planet, with a diameter of about 31,770 miles (51,118 km). It is a near-twin of Neptune both in size and in composition—both have deep atmospheres with warm oceans beneath. But they differ in one important respect. Neptune spins around in space more or less upright as it orbits the Sun, but Uranus has its axis tilted right over, so it is nearly spinning on its side.

Almost featureless atmosphere

Methane colors the atmosphere blue-green

DEEP-SPACE EXPLORER
Most of our detailed knowledge about the twin planets Uranus and Neptune has come from the *Voyager 2* probe. Launched in 1977, it spent 12 years visiting the four gas-giant planets. After Jupiter and Saturn, it sped past Uranus in 1986 and Neptune three years later. By the time it reached Neptune, *Voyager 2* had journeyed for 4.4 billion miles (7 billion km)—and it was still working perfectly.

Cameras

Science instruments

Dish antenna

Magnetometer boom

Miranda

Tracklike surfaces

Cracked crust

Hydrogen and helium are the main gases in the atmosphere

CRAZED MOONS
Uranus has at least 27 moons. Made up of rock and ice, they are all distinctly different. Ariel has deep cracks running across its surface. Miranda has all kinds of different surface features mixed together. Some astronomers think this moon once broke apart, then came together again.

Ariel

Dark spots are lower in atmosphere than bright, high-speed "scooters"

BLUE PLANET

Neptune lies 1 billion miles (1.6 billion km) beyond Uranus. It is slightly smaller than its inner neighbor, with a diameter of 30,780 miles (49,532 km) and has a fainter ring system. The atmosphere is flecked with bright clouds and sometimes with dark oval storm regions, and is bluer than Uranus because it contains more methane. *Voyager 2* recorded a huge storm there in 1989. For Neptune to have so much atmospheric activity, it must have some kind of internal heating. This heat also keeps Neptune's cloud tops at the same temperature as Uranus's, even though it is very much farther from the Sun.

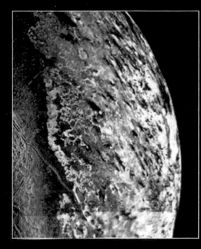

Temperature at cloud tops -345°F (-210°C)

TRITON'S GEYSERS

Triton is by far the largest of Neptune's thirteen moons, 1,680 miles (2,710 km) across. It is a deep-frozen world, similar to Pluto, and both are probably large members of a swarm of icy bodies that orbits beyond Neptune. Triton's surface is covered with frozen nitrogen and methane and, amazingly, has geysers erupting on it. The geysers don't spurt out steam and water, of course, but nitrogen gas and dust.

FINDING NEPTUNE

Johann Galle first observed Neptune in 1846 after French mathematician Urbain Leverrier (1811–1877) had calculated where it should be found. John Couch Adams (1819–1892) of England had made similar calculations a year earlier, but no one had acted upon them.

RÉPUBLIQUE FRANÇAISE
POSTES 12 F
1811 LE VERRIER 1877

Uranus has a total of 11 rings around its equator

Ring particles average about 3 ft (1 m) across

Charon circles around Pluto every 6 days 9 hours

Outer ring is brightest

ICY OUTCASTS

Pluto has been classed as a dwarf planet since 2006. It is smaller than Earth's moon, measuring only 1,413 miles (2,274 km) across. It has three moons of its own—Charon which is half its size and tiny Nix and Hydra. Pluto is made up of rock and ice, with frozen nitrogen and methane covering its surface. For 20 years of Pluto's 248-year orbit it travels closer to the Sun than Neptune. Pluto was last inside Neptune's orbit in 1999.

Pluto lies on average 3,670 miles (5,900 million km) from the Sun

Asteroids, meteors, and meteorites

THE SOLAR SYSTEM has many members besides planets, dwarf planets, and moons. The largest are the rocky lumps we call asteroids, orbiting relatively close to the Sun. Swarms of smaller icy bodies lurk much farther away, at the edge of the solar system. Some occasionally travel in toward the Sun, where they warm up, release clouds of gas and dust, and become visible as comets (p. 40). Asteroids often collide and chip pieces off one another, and comets leave trails of dust in their wake. Asteroid and comet particles, called meteoroids, exist in interplanetary space. When they cross Earth's orbit and enter its atmosphere, most burn up in the atmosphere as shooting stars, also termed meteors. Those that survive the journey through the atmosphere and reach the ground are called meteorites.

Asteroid Ida

THE ASTEROID BELT
About 200,000 individual asteroids have been identified but there are billions altogether. Most of them circle the Sun in a broad band roughly midway between the orbits of Mars and Jupiter. We call this band the Asteroid Belt. The center of the belt lies roughly 250 million miles (400 million km) from the Sun. Some asteroids, however, stray outside the belt, following orbits that can take them inside Earth's orbit or out beyond Saturn's.

ASTEROID VARIETY
Even the largest asteroid, Ceres, is only about 580 miles (930 km) across, which makes it less than one-third the size of the Moon. The next largest, Pallas and Vesta, are only about half the size of Ceres. But most asteroids are very much smaller—Ida, for example, is about 35 miles (56 km) long; Gaspra only about 11 miles (18 km). These were the first asteroids photographed, by the *Galileo* spacecraft on its way to Jupiter. Gaspra is made up mostly of silicate rocks, like many asteroids. Ida's structure is more of a mystery. Other asteroids are mainly metal, or a mixture of rock and metal.

Sample of nickel-iron meteorite

THE CELESTIAL POLICE
In 1800, Hungarian baron Franz von Zach organized a search party of German astronomers to look for a planet in the apparent "gap" in the solar system between Mars and Jupiter. They became known as the Celestial Police. But they were upstaged by Italian astronomer Giuseppe Piazzi, who spotted a new "planet" in the gap on January 1, 1801. Named Ceres, it was the first asteroid and in 2006 was also classed as a dwarf planet.

Giuseppe Piazzi
(1746–1826)

ASTEROID MINING
The metallic asteroids are rich in iron, as well as nickel and other metals that are comparatively rare on Earth. Metals in asteroids exist in pure form, not in ores as on Earth, and this makes them much easier to extract. So when supplies of these rarer metals start to run out, we might send astronauts or robotic mining machines into space to mine the asteroids and send their materials back to Earth. Near-Earth asteroids—the ones that come closest to our planet—would be the first targets.

Eros

NEAR-
Shoemaker
spacecraft

NEAR EROS
In February 2001, the probe *NEAR-Shoemaker* performed a remarkable feat. It landed on the asteroid Eros, a rocky lump only about 20 miles (33 km) long. *NEAR* (the Near-Earth Asteroid Rendezvous) had already orbited the asteroid for a year.

SHOWERS OF METEORS
The short-lived streaks of light we see in the night sky are meteors. They are produced by meteoroid particles usually little bigger than sand grains. As they move through the atmosphere the particles cause the gas atoms in the atmosphere to glow. On average, up to about 10 meteors can be seen in the night sky every hour. But during meteor showers and storms, thousands may be seen.

The 1833 Leonid meteor storm over Niagara Falls

Ida's deeply gouged surface probably formed as it broke up from a larger asteroid millions of years ago

Meteorites stand out in a rockless landscape

NASA's NOMAD robot is designed to hunt for meteorites in hostile regions

Gaspra has fewer craters than Ida—it probably also formed in a breakup

Asteroid Gaspra

LOOKING FOR METEORITES
The southern continent of Antarctica has provided rich pickings for hunters of meteorites—meteoroid lumps that have survived passage through the atmosphere. A combination of ice movements and harsh winds causes meteorites scattered over a wide area to accumulate in certain places.

Crater rim is filled with a lake now used as a reservoir

Crater floor may hide huge nickel deposits

Manicouagan crater, Quebec

Micrograph showing crystals in a stony meteorite.

INSIDE METEORITES
Most of the meteorites that have been recovered are made up of stony material. But all the biggest ones are made up of metal, mainly iron and nickel. The giant Hoba West meteorite found in Namibia weighs at least 60 tons. Some meteorites are rich in carbon compounds, which form the building blocks of life.

METEOR CRATERS
From time to time, really big meteorites smash into Earth's surface and gouge out large pits, or craters. 200 million years ago, a big meteorite created this crater in Canada, which has since filled with ice. The best-preserved crater is Meteor Crater in the arid Arizona desert, formed around 50,000 years ago. It measures about 4,150 ft (1,265 m) across and 575 ft (175 m) deep.

Icy wanderers

IN THE OUTER REACHES of the solar system, there are great clouds of icy debris, relics of the time the solar system was born. Each of these chunks is the city-sized nucleus of a comet; a dirty-snowball that remains invisible unless it travels in toward the Sun and is heated up. It then develops a large head and tails and is big enough and close enough to be seen. At their brightest, comets can rival the brightest planets, and can develop tails that stretch for millions of miles. Comets seem suddenly to appear out of nowhere. In the past, people believed they were signs of ill-omen, and brought famine, disease, death, and destruction.

HAPPY RETURNS
In his famous painting *Adoration of the Magi*, the Florentine painter Giotto (1267–1337) included a comet as the Star of Bethlehem, based on one he had seen in 1301. Giotto's comet was in fact one of the regular appearances of Halley's Comet, whose orbit brings it close to the Sun once every 76 years. The comet has been spotted on every return since 240 BCE.

Gas plume bursts out of surface

HEART OF A COMET
In March 1986, the space probe *Giotto* took spectacular close-up pictures of Halley's Comet. They showed bright jets of gas spurting out of the central nucleus. Shaped a bit like a potato, it measures about 10 miles (16 km) long and about half as big across. The surface is rough, covered with what look like hills and craters. It is also very dark. Analysis of the gases coming off showed them to be 80 percent water vapor. There were also traces of carbon-based organic compounds, and some astronomers think that comets might distribute these building blocks of life around the galaxy.

Straight gas tail streams away, driven by solar wind

Dark dust coats nucleus

Gas tail glows as solar wind strikes gas from comet

Dark surface absorbs heat from sunlight

Nucleus is too small to be seen inside comet's glowing coma

FRAGILE SNOWBALLS
Like snowballs, comets are not firmly held together and often break up. Early in July 1992, a comet passed very close to Jupiter and was ripped apart by the giant planet's gravity. The following spring, the fragments were spotted by comet-watchers Carolyn and Gene Shoemaker and David Levy. It soon became evident that this fragmented comet, called Shoemaker-Levy 9, was going to collide with Jupiter, which it did in July 1994.

COMET OF THE CENTURY
In spring 1997, Earth's sky was dominated by one of the brightest comets of the 20th century. It had been discovered by US astronomers Alan Hale and Thomas Bopp two years earlier. Comet Hale-Bopp outshone all but the brightest stars and hung in the night sky for weeks. It had two well-developed tails streaming away from the bright head, or coma. There was a curved, yellowish dust tail and a straighter blue gas, or ion tail. Hale-Bopp's nucleus is estimated to be 20–30 miles (30–40 km) across.

Orbit of Saturn

COMET ORBITS

Comets travel in orbits around the Sun just like the planets. But they do not usually orbit in the same plane—they may journey in toward the Sun from any direction. For much of the time, they remain in deep freeze. Only when they get inside Saturn's orbit do they begin to warm up and start to glow. As they get closer to the Sun, their tails start to form, always pointing away from the Sun.

Tail follows comet as it approaches Sun

Tail leads comet as it recedes from Sun

Orbit of Uranus

Short-period comet from Kuiper Belt orbits in a few decades

Orbit of Neptune

Long-period comet from Oort Cloud orbits in centuries or more

EDMOND HALLEY

English astronomer Edmond Halley (1656–1742) was the first to discover that some comets are regular visitors to Earth's skies. He observed a comet in 1682, and after checking the orbits of previous comets, he deduced that it was the same one that had appeared in 1531 and 1607. He predicted that it would return again in 1758. When the comet reappeared as forecast, it was named after him—usually, a comet is named after the person who first discovers it.

Edm.d Halley A.P.R.

Dust tail curves, affected by Sun's gravity

Dust tail is simply comet dust reflecting sunlight

COMET RESERVOIRS

Comets journey in toward the Sun from the outer reaches of the solar system, where there are great reservoirs of icy bodies. Many come from the Kuiper Belt, a region stretching for 2 billion miles (3 billion km) or more beyond the orbit of Neptune. Others arrive from much farther afield—from the Oort Cloud, a spherical shell containing trillions of comets. The Cloud extends out to 9.4 trillion miles (15 trillion km) from the Sun.

THE TUNGUSKA EVENT

On the last day of June 1908, a terrifying explosion occurred in Siberia near the Stony Tunguska River. It generated a dazzling fireball and shock waves reminiscent of a thermonuclear blast. In an instant, 60,000 trees lay flattened and charred. No one knows for sure what caused the event, but astronomers think it was probably part of a comet nucleus impacting the atmosphere at high speed and exploding 4 miles (6 km) above the ground.

Distant suns

EVERY CLEAR NIGHT, if you were very patient, you could probably count as many as 2,500 stars in the sky. Through binoculars or a small telescope, you could see millions more. They always appear as tiny, faint pinpricks of light, but if you traveled trillions of miles to look at them close up, you would find that they are huge, bright bodies like the Sun. Even the closest star (Proxima Centauri) lies so far away that its light takes over four years to reach us—we say that it lies over four light-years away. Astronomers often use the light-year—the distance light travels in a year—as a unit to measure distances to stars. They also use a unit called the parsec, which equals about 3.3 light-years.

A UNIVERSE OF STARS
In the dense star clouds of the Milky Way, stars appear crammed together in their millions. There are many different kinds of stars, with different brightness, color, size, and mass. Altogether in our own great galaxy—a "star island" in space—there are as many as 500 billion stars. And there are billions more galaxies like it in the universe.

Stars of the Sagittarius Star Cloud

Star Cloud lies 25,000 light-years from Earth, toward the center of the Milky Way

Gamma Cassiopeiae (615 light-years)

Epsilon Cassiopeiae (440 light-years)

Alpha Cassiopeiae (240 light-years)

Beta Cassiopeiae (54 light-years)

True distances to Cassiopeia's stars (not to scale)

Delta Cassiopeiae (100 light-years)

Star pattern in the constellation Cassiopeia

STARS AND CONSTELLATIONS
Some of the bright stars form patterns in the sky that we can recognize. We call them the constellations. Ancient astronomers named them after figures that featured in their myths and legends. The stars in the constellations look as if they are the same distance from Earth, but actually are far apart. They appear together only because they happen to lie in the same direction in space. This also means that stars that seem to have the same brightness may, in fact, be very different.

HOW FAR AWAY?
The distance to a few hundred of the nearest stars can be measured directly by the parallax method. Parallax is the effect that makes a nearby object appear to move against a more distant background when you look at it first with one eye, then the other. Astronomers view a nearby star first from one side of Earth's orbit, then from the other. They measure the amount a star appears to move against the background of more distant stars. From these parallax shifts they can work out the star's distance.

Closer star B has larger parallax shift than more distant star A

Distant stars

Parallax shift against distant background stars

Line of sight to star B

Line of sight to star A

Earth's position in January

Earth's position in July

Sun

Betelgeuse (magnitude 0.8)

Rigel and Betelgeuse appear roughly the same brightness, but Rigel is really twice as far away and five times more luminous than Betelgeuse.

Rigel (magnitude 0.1)

STAR BRIGHTNESS
The stars in the constellations differ widely in brightness, as here in Orion. We measure brightness on a scale of magnitude introduced by the Greek astronomer Hipparchus over 2,000 years ago. He graded the brightest stars we can see as first-magnitude stars, and the dimmest ones as sixth-magnitude. Today, we extend the scale to negative magnitudes for very bright stars, and beyond 6 for stars too faint for the eye to detect.

More massive star
pulls material off
its neighbor

Stars of Algol
are very close
together

Artist's impression of
Algol star system

BINARY STARS
Most stars travel through space with one or more
companions. Two-star, or binary, systems are
common. Each star orbits around an imaginary
point, called the barycenter, that marks the center
of mass of the system. The two components in a
binary system may orbit very close together and
appear as a single star to the eye, but they can
often be seen separately in a telescope. When they
are really close together, they can be separated
only by studying their spectrum.

Sodium absorption and emission lines

THE SPECTRAL LINES
The dark lines in a star's spectrum are produced when certain
wavelengths are removed from starlight by elements in the
star's atmosphere. Sodium, for example, removes wavelengths
in the yellow region of the spectrum (top picture). It is the same
wavelength that sodium itself would emit if it were
heated (lower picture).

Sagittarius region is
rich in old red and
yellow stars

SPECTROSCOPY
The white light we receive from the stars (and the Sun)
is actually made up of a mixture of different colors, or
wavelengths. Using an instrument called a spectroscope,
we can split starlight into its separate colors to form
a rainbowlike spectrum. Dark lines cross the
spectrum at intervals. By studying these spectral
lines, astronomers can tell all kinds of things
about a star, such as its composition,
temperature, color, true brightness, and
even how fast it is moving.

Spectroscope
attaches to end of a
telescope here

Screws allow
adjustment of
viewing angle

Eyepiece for
viewing magnified
spectrum and
identifying lines

Scale allows
measurement of
position being
viewed

An antique
spectroscope

Prism or grating
splits light into a
spectrum

ANNIE JUMP CANNON
US astronomer Annie Jump Cannon
(1863–1941) pioneered the classification
of stellar spectra. Her work on some
300,000 stars established that stars
of different colors contain different
chemicals, and led to the division of the
stars into different spectral types.

The variety of stars

STUDYING THE SPECTRA of stars tells us all kinds of things about them—their composition, color, temperature, speed of travel, and size. Other techniques allow astronomers to measure the distance to stars and their mass. Stars turn out to vary enormously. There are dwarfs with only a hundredth the diameter of the Sun and supergiants hundreds of times the Sun's size. The lightest stars have around one-tenth of the Sun's mass, the heaviest around 50 solar masses. The least luminous are a million times fainter than the Sun, while the most luminous are a million times brighter. But there do seem to be some rules—red stars are either very faint or very luminous, while the bluer a star, the more luminous it is.

STARS LARGE AND SMALL
A range of typical stars is shown across this page. The most luminous are at the top, the hottest on the left, and the coolest on the right. The true size differences are far greater than those shown, but some patterns are obvious—stars get bigger as luminosity increases, and the most luminous are either bright blue or orange-red. A star's color is governed by its surface temperature— the amount of energy pumping out of each square meter of its surface. This means that if two stars have the same luminosity but one is cool and red while the other is hot and blue, then the red one must be far bigger than the blue one.

SUPERGIANTS
The biggest stars of all, hundreds of millions of miles across, relatively cool but amazingly luminous

BLUE STARS
Tens of times bigger than the Sun, and tens of thousands of times more luminous, with a surface temperature up to 90,000°F (50,000°C)

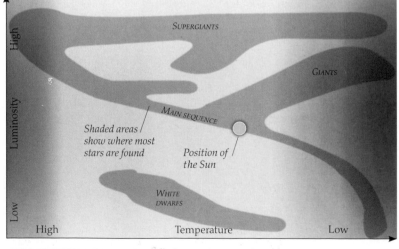

THE HERTZSPRUNG-RUSSELL DIAGRAM AND STELLAR EVOLUTION
The Hertzsprung-Russell (HR) diagram is a way of looking at relationships between the luminosity (amount of light produced) of stars and their color and temperature. The majority of stars lie along a diagonal strip from faint red to bright blue called the main sequence—this must be where most stars spend most of their lives. Stars spend much of their lives close to one point on the main sequence—they only move off it toward the end of their lives, as they grow bigger and more luminous.

WHITE DWARFS
Tiny hot stars only about the size of Earth

Line of main sequence

FIRST DWARF
Stars similar to the Sun end their lives as white dwarfs, which gradually fade away. The faint companion of Sirius, called Sirius B (left), was the first white dwarf discovered, by US astronomer Alvan Clark in 1862. It proved to be exceptionally hot and very dense.

The most luminous supergiants are a million times brighter than the Sun

Star at its hottest causes outward expansion

Star at its coolest collapses back under gravity

Star oscillates back and forth through balance point

Star is brightest when at its hottest

Size and color change is exaggerated

PULSATING VARIABLES
Not all stars shine steadily. Some change in brightness—we call them variables. Pulsating variables alter their brightness as they pulsate, getting periodically bigger then smaller. They are brightest when they are small and hot, dimmest when they are large and cool. These variables are stars near the end of their lives, like the red giant star Mira.

Bright star eclipsed

Dim star eclipsed

Combined star at its brightest

Brightness drops dramatically

Brightness drops slightly

ECLIPSING VARIABLES
Eclipsing variables appear to vary in brightness for another reason. They are binary star systems in which a small bright star and a large dim star orbit around each other. They orbit in our line of sight so that each passes in front of, or eclipses, the other in turn. When this happens, the overall brightness of the system dips.

Perseus used his shield to look at Medusa when he confronted her

THE WINKING DEMON
In the constellation Perseus, a variable star named Algol marks the eye of Medusa, the snake-haired Gorgon that the Greek hero slew. Algol, often called the winking demon, dips noticeably in brightness every 2.9 days. English astronomer John Goodricke first recognized that it was an eclipsing binary in 1783.

Medusa's gaze could turn people to stone

RED GIANTS
Luminous stars, but cool because of their size, typically about 30 times the size of the Sun

RED DWARFS
About one-tenth of the size of the Sun, with a surface temperature of about 3,000°C (5,500°F)

SUNLIKE STARS
Roughly 900,000 miles (1,500,000 km) across, with a surface temperature of around 11,000°F (6,000°C)

The faintest red dwarfs are a million times less luminous than our Sun

SUNLIKE STARS
The Sun is an average star of a type known as a yellow dwarf. Its color reflects its surface temperature, which is around 9,900°F (5,500°C). Astronomers think that the Sun is about halfway through its life, which means that it should stay on the main sequence, shining steadily, for another 5 billion years.

EJNAR HERTZSPRUNG
Ejnar Hertzsprung (1873–1967) was born in Frederiksberg, Denmark. He studied to be a chemical engineer but became an astronomer instead. He first noticed the relationship between star brightness and temperature in 1906. Working in the US, Henry Norris Russell (1877–1957) independently came to similar conclusions. Both are commemorated in the HR diagram, which is of vital importance in astronomy.

Clusters and nebulae

IN MANY PARTS OF THE HEAVENS there are fuzzy patches that look as if they might be comets. Through a telescope, some turn out to be close groupings of stars, known as clusters—in general, stars are born in groups rather than alone. Open clusters are relatively loose collections of a few hundred stars. Globular clusters are dense groupings of many thousands of stars. Other fuzzy patches turn out to be cloudlike regions of glowing gas. We call these nebulae, from the Latin word for clouds. They are the visible part of the interstellar medium, the stuff that occupies the space between the stars. The darker, denser parts of nebulae are where stars are born.

Alcyone

OPEN CLUSTERS
The best-known of all open clusters is the Pleiades, in the constellation Taurus. It is also called the Seven Sisters because keen-sighted people can make out its seven brightest stars with the naked eye, and sometimes the sisters' parents, Atlas and Pleione. In total, the Pleiades contains more than stars, all of them hot, blue and young— probably less than 80 million years old. Most open clusters contain similar kinds of stars.

Pleione

Atlas

The spectacular globular cluster Omega Centauri

GLOBES OF STARS
Globular clusters are made up of hundreds of thousands of stars packed together in a ball. They contain mostly ancient stars, typically about 10 billion years old. While open clusters are found among the stars in the disk of our galaxy, globular clusters lie in the center and in a spherical halo above and below the disk. They follow their own orbits around the central bulge.

Merope

Between the stars

The interstellar medium is made up mainly of hydrogen gas and specks of dust. It also contains traces of many other compounds, including water, alcohol, hydrogen sulfide, and ammonia. Altogether, the interstellar medium accounts for a one-tenth of the mass of our galaxy. It can become visible as both bright and dark nebulae.

Asterope

Taygeta

Maia

Celaeno

Electra

DARK NEBULAE
Some clouds of gas and dust are lit up, while others remain dark. We see dark nebulae only when they blot out the light from stars or glowing gas in the background. The aptly named Horsehead Nebula (above) is a well-known dark nebula in Orion. Another, in far southern skies, is the Coal Sack in Crux, the Southern Cross. Dark nebulae are generally cold, around -436°F (-260°C), and made up mainly of hydrogen molecules. Such molecular clouds give birth to stars.

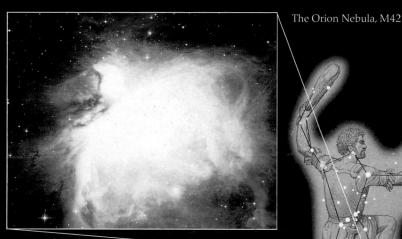

The Orion Nebula, M42

M42's position in Orion

BRIGHT NEBULAE
Many interstellar gas clouds are lit up by stars, creating some of the most beautiful sights in the heavens. Sometimes the clouds just reflect the light from nearby stars, and we see them as reflection nebulae. Sometimes radiation from stars embedded within the clouds gives extra energy to the gas molecules, causing them to emit radiation. Then we see the clouds as emission nebulae. The famous Orion Nebula (above) is primarily an emission nebula.

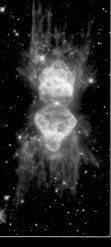

STELLAR REMNANTS
Stars are born from nebulae, and give rise to nebulae when they die. Stars like the Sun first swell up to become red giants, then shrink into tiny white dwarfs. As they do so, they puff off layers of gas, which become planetary nebulae. Some of these nebulae are circular and look a little like the disks of planets; others, like the Ant Nebula, consist of luminous jets.

Reflection nebula surrounding young stars

MESSIER'S CATALOG
French astronomer Charles Messier (1730–1817) was nicknamed the "ferret of comets" for his skill in searching for new comets. He discovered 15 in all. He also compiled a catalog in which he listed 104 star clusters and nebulae that might be mistaken for comets. The objects in the catalog are still often identified by their Messier (M) numbers.

Star birth

Central core heats up

Matter spirals in

STARS ARE BORN in the vast, dark fogs of gas and dust that occupy interstellar space. Called giant molecular clouds, they are very cold (around -436°F, -260°C) and consist mainly of hydrogen gas. In places within these clouds, gravity pulls the gas molecules together to make denser clumps. Within these clumps there are even denser regions, called cores, and it is from cores that individual stars are born. Gravity makes a core collapse in on itself, greatly compressing the material at the center. As the collapse continues, the central region becomes more and more compressed and gets hotter and hotter. Now called a protostar, it begins to glow. When its temperature reaches around 18 million°F (10 million°C), its nuclear furnace fires up, and it begins to shine brightly as a new star.

IN A WHIRL
The molecular clouds that spawn stars move around slowly in space. When cores of matter collapse during star formation, they start to rotate—the smaller they become, the faster they spin. The collapsing matter, with the glowing protostar inside, forms into a disk as a result of the rotation.

STELLAR NURSERIES
Stars are being born in vast numbers in giant molecular clouds all around the heavens. M16, the Eagle Nebula in Serpens, is one of these stellar nurseries. The Hubble Space Telescope has taken dramatic pictures of dark columns nicknamed "the pillars of creation," where star formation is taking place. This picture of the top of one pillar shows fingerlike blobs of gas called EGGs, or evaporating gaseous globules where material is collapsing to form stars.

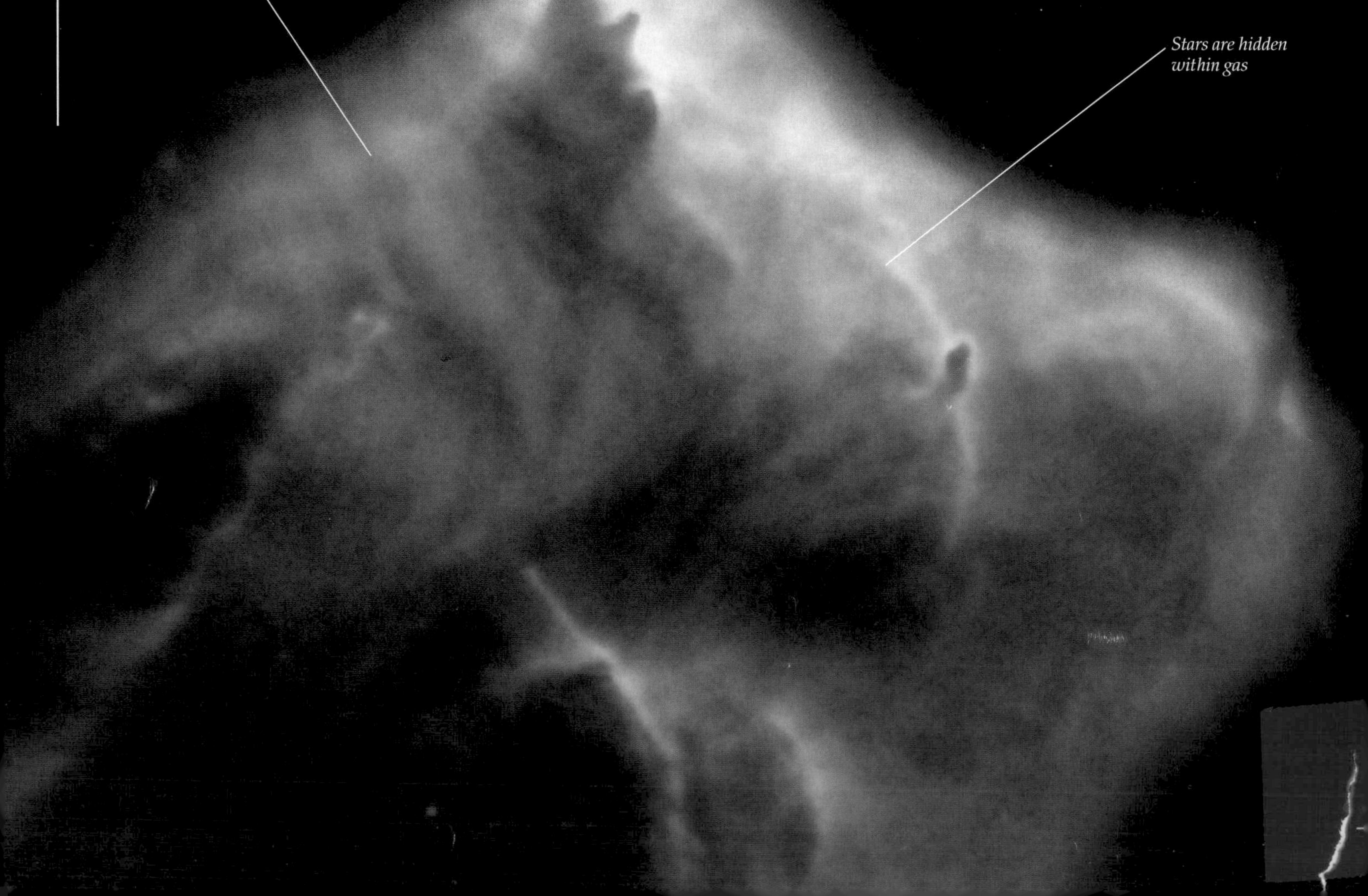

Collapsing gas clouds

EGG

Stars are hidden within gas

Disk more stable at greater distances from star

Close to star, matter is pulled in by gravity

Stellar winds blow material out in jets

Disk heats up close to star

BIRTH PANGS
A newborn star is surrounded by a swirling disk of matter with may be three times its mass, but not for long. Powerful stellar winds gather up the matter and force it away from the star's poles as twin jets. This is called bipolar outflow.

JET EFFECTS
The two jets that emerge from the poles of newborn stars travel very fast—at speeds of hundreds of miles a second. As they punch their way through interstellar gas, they make it glow, creating what are called Herbig-Haro Objects. The picture shows one close to the young star Gamma Cassiopeiae.

Sulfur ions glow blue when jet hits them

Central star

Nearby gas reflecting starlight

Hydrogen atoms glow green when struck by jet

Worlds beyond

Newborn stars blow most of the matter surrounding them into space, but usually a disk of material remains. It is from such disks that planetary systems form. Astronomers first began discovering planets around ordinary stars in 1995. Today, we know of more than 300 of these extrasolar planets, or exoplanets.

Star blacked out

Disk seen edge-on to Earth

THE HIDDEN MILLIONS
The Orion Nebula is one of the closest star-forming regions. In visible light (above left), glowing gas in the nebula hides most of the young stars. But viewed in the infrared (above right), a wealth of stars becomes visible, many of them red and brown dwarfs. Red dwarfs are small, cool stars. Brown dwarfs are the stars that never made it. They have a low mass and couldn't reach a high enough temperature for nuclear fusion to begin.

Disk of gas and dust

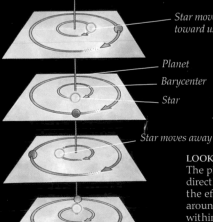

Star moves toward us

Planet

Barycenter

Star

Star moves away

PLANETS IN FORMATION
Space probes like *IRAS* (Infrared Astronomy Satellite) began detecting disks of material around other stars in the 1980s. One is Beta Pictoris, which is pictured above. Another is the bright star Vega in Lyra. Planets could form in these systems within a few million years.

LOOKING FOR PLANETS
The planets around other stars are much too faint to be seen directly. Astronomers have to find them indirectly, by observing the effect they have on their star. Planet and star both orbit around a shared center of gravity or barycenter, usually deep within the star but not quite at the center. During an orbit, the star appears from Earth to move repeatedly toward and away from us. We can detect this motion by examining the shift in the lines in the star's spectrum (p .42).

GIANTS LIKE JUPITER
Astronomers detected the first extrasolar planets in 1991, orbiting a dead star called a pulsar. Four years later, a planet was found around the Sunlike 51 Pegasi. It has half the mass of Jupiter and orbits only about 6 million miles (10 million km) from its star. Most exoplanets detected so far are heavier than Jupiter, and orbit close to their stars.

Star death

STARS BURST INTO LIFE when they begin fusing hydrogen into helium in nuclear reactions in their cores. They spend most of their lives shining steadily until they use up their hydrogen fuel—then they start to die. First they pass through a phase when they brighten and swell to enormous size as red giants and supergiants. The way a star ultimately dies depends on its mass. Low-mass stars puff off their outer layers and then fade away. High-mass stars die in a spectacular explosion called a supernova.

LIVE FAST, DIE YOUNG
Stars more massive than the Sun have hotter, denser cores. This allows them to burn their hydrogen fuel in a much more efficient way, but also shortens their lifespans dramatically—the heaviest are stable for just a few million years.

New fusion reactions produce sodium, magnesium, silicon, sulfur, and other elements

Heaviest element produced is iron

Core not shown to scale

Core develops "onion layers"

FATES OF STARS
A star that is burning hydrogen in its core changes its color and brightness very little. How long the star can keep burning hydrogen depends on its mass. Stars like the Sun burn their fuel slowly and so can shine steadily for up to 10 billion years.

RED GIANT
When a star has used up the hydrogen in its core, fusion moves out to a thin shell around the center. This produces so much heat that the star's atmosphere balloons outward. As it expands, its surface cools and its light reddens—it has become a red giant. Meanwhile, the inner core of helium collapses, until it is hot and dense enough for new nuclear reactions to begin. These turn helium into heavier elements and give the star a new lease of life—for about 2 billion years.

SUPERGIANT
In stars with more than eight times the Sun's mass, the core gets so hot that carbon and oxygen, produced by helium fusion, can themselves fuse into heavier elements. The star balloons out to become a supergiant, many times larger than a normal red giant.

PLANETARY NEBULA
When all the helium in the core of a solar-mass red giant runs out, the core collapses again, releasing energy that blows the outer layers of the star into space. Radiation from the hot core makes the ejected gas light up, forming a ring-shaped planetary nebula.

Black hole

END STATES
What survives after a supernova depends on the mass of the collapsing core. If the core has less than about three solar masses, it will shrink to an incredibly dense neutron star. If the core has a greater mass, it will end up as a black hole and vanish forever from the visible universe (p.52).

Neutron star

SUPERNOVA
Iron builds up rapidly in a supergiant's core—it cannot be burned by nuclear reactions in the same way as lighter elements.

When the core runs out of other fuel, it cannot support itself and suddenly collapses. So much energy is released that the star blasts itself apart in a supernova explosion that can briefly outshine an entire galaxy. The explosion scatters heavy elements across space, providing material for later generations of stars and planets.

SUPERNOVA 1987A
On February 23, 1987, astronomers spotted a bright supernova (left) in the Large Magellanic Cloud, one of the closest galaxies to our own. It flared up over 85 days to become easily visible to the naked eye. The star that exploded was a blue giant called Sanduleak -69°202 (far left), with about 20 times the mass of the Sun.

SUPERNOVAE IN HISTORY
Tycho Brahe saw a supernova in 1572 (shown above), which caused him to realize that the heavens were not unchanging. But the most famous historical supernova is probably the one Chinese astronomers saw in 1054; today its remains form the Crab Nebula in the constellation Taurus.

WHITE DWARF
Within a planetary nebula, the star's core continues collapsing until the electrons in its atoms are forced up against the central nuclei. It is now about the same size as Earth, and a matchbox of its material would weigh as much as an elephant. This incredibly dense, hot star is called a white dwarf. It is very difficult to see because of its tiny size.

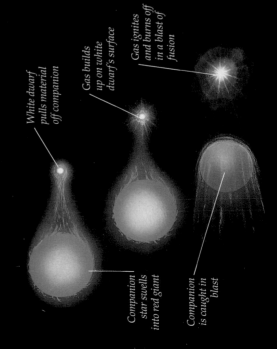

White dwarf pulls material off companion

Companion star swells into red giant

Gas builds up on white dwarf's surface

Gas ignites and burns off in a blast of fusion

Companion is caught in blast

NOVAE
When a white dwarf forms in a close binary star system, it may attract gas from the other star. Over time, gas builds up on the white dwarf's surface until it is hot and dense enough to trigger nuclear fusion. A gigantic explosion takes place that makes the star flare up and makes the star flare up, an apparently new star.

Pulsars and black holes

W<small>HEN A MASSIVE STAR DIES</small> in a supernova (p. 50), only the core is left behind, collapsed under its own enormous gravity. The force as the core collapses is so great that atoms are broken down. Negatively charged electrons are forced into the central nucleus of each atom, combining with positively charged protons to turn all the matter into tightly packed neutrons that have no electric charge. The collapsed core becomes a city-sized neutron star, spinning furiously as it emits pulses of radiation. When we detect the pulses from a neutron star, we call it a pulsar. Collapsing cores with more than three solar masses suffer a different fate. The force of collapse is so great that even neutrons get crushed. Eventually, the core is so dense that not even light can escape its gravity—it has become that most mysterious of bodies, a black hole.

THE CRAB PULSAR
In the year 1054, Chinese astronomers recorded seeing a star in the constellation Taurus bright enough to be visible in daylight. We now know that it was a supernova explosion, which created the famous Crab Nebula. Buried inside the nebula is the collapsed core, which we detect as a pulsar.

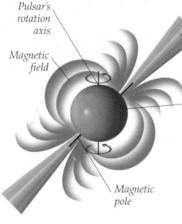

Pulsar's rotation axis

Magnetic field

Jets from magnetic poles

Neutron star

Magnetic pole

Inner ring one light-year across

INSIDE THE CRAB
The pulsar in the Crab Nebula has been closely studied. It spins around 30 times a second and pours out energy not only as radio waves but also as visible light and X-rays. This picture combines an X-ray image from the Chandra X-ray Observatory satellite (in blue) with a visible light photo.

Jet from pulsar poles

Pulsar jet billows into clouds as it contacts interstellar gas

Material blown out from equator reaches half the speed of light

Neutron star

NEUTRON STARS
Neutron stars are tiny bodies that spin around rapidly. The fastest one known spins 1,122 times a second. They are highly magnetic, so their magnetic field sweeps around rapidly as well. This generates radio waves, which are emitted as beams from the magnetic poles. When the beams sweep past Earth, we see them as pulsing signals, a bit like the flashes from a lighthouse.

SUPERDENSE MATTER
A neutron star is typically only around 12 miles (20 km) across. Yet it contains the mass of up to three Suns. This makes it incredibly dense. Just a pinhead of neutron-star matter would weigh twice as much as the world's heaviest supertanker. It is unlike any kind of matter found on Earth.

PULSAR DISCOVERY
Working at Cambridge University in 1967, astronomy research student Jocelyn Bell Burnell (born 1943) was testing new equipment to study fluctuating radio sources. On August 6, she picked up signals pulsating every 1.337 seconds. It was the first pulsar to be found, now called PSR 1919+21.

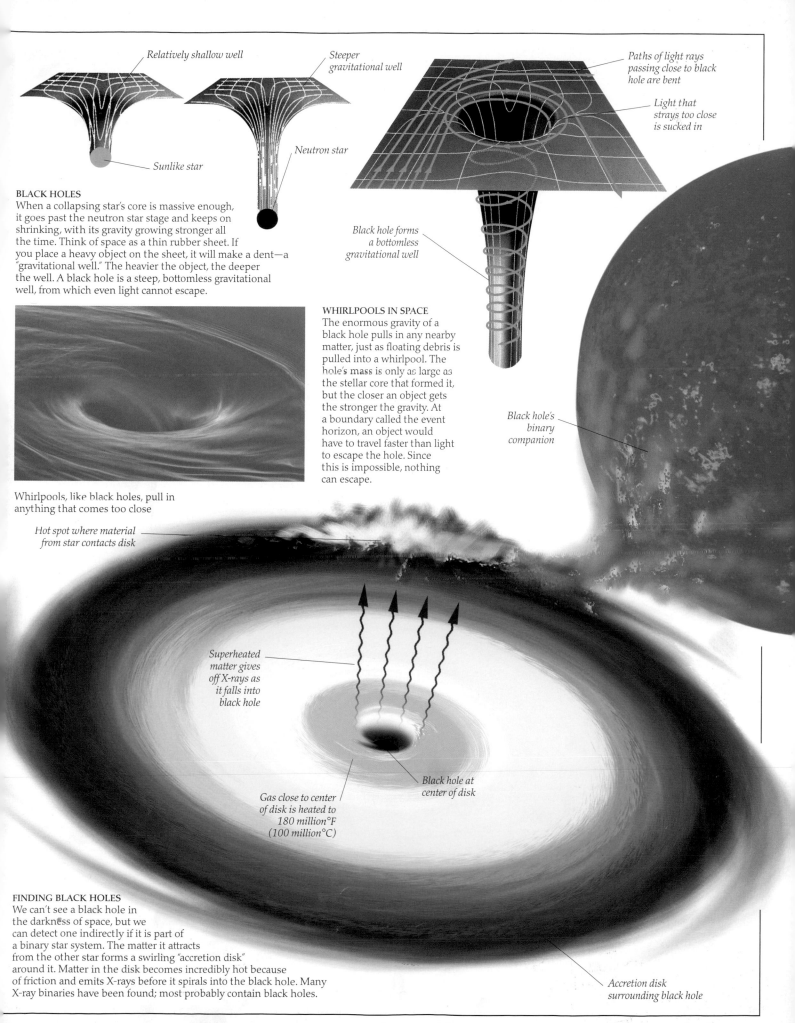

Relatively shallow well

Steeper gravitational well

Paths of light rays passing close to black hole are bent

Light that strays too close is sucked in

Sunlike star

Neutron star

BLACK HOLES

When a collapsing star's core is massive enough, it goes past the neutron star stage and keeps on shrinking, with its gravity growing stronger all the time. Think of space as a thin rubber sheet. If you place a heavy object on the sheet, it will make a dent—a "gravitational well." The heavier the object, the deeper the well. A black hole is a steep, bottomless gravitational well, from which even light cannot escape.

Black hole forms a bottomless gravitational well

WHIRLPOOLS IN SPACE

The enormous gravity of a black hole pulls in any nearby matter, just as floating debris is pulled into a whirlpool. The hole's mass is only as large as the stellar core that formed it, but the closer an object gets the stronger the gravity. At a boundary called the event horizon, an object would have to travel faster than light to escape the hole. Since this is impossible, nothing can escape.

Black hole's binary companion

Whirlpools, like black holes, pull in anything that comes too close

Hot spot where material from star contacts disk

Superheated matter gives off X-rays as it falls into black hole

Black hole at center of disk

Gas close to center of disk is heated to 180 million°F (100 million°C)

FINDING BLACK HOLES

We can't see a black hole in the darkness of space, but we can detect one indirectly if it is part of a binary star system. The matter it attracts from the other star forms a swirling "accretion disk" around it. Matter in the disk becomes incredibly hot because of friction and emits X-rays before it spirals into the black hole. Many X-ray binaries have been found; most probably contain black holes.

Accretion disk surrounding black hole

The Milky Way

ON A CLEAR, DARK NIGHT, a faint, hazy band of light arches across the heavens, running through many of the best-known constellations. We call it the Milky Way. What we are seeing is a kind of "slice" through the star system, or galaxy, to which the Sun and all the other stars in the sky belong. It passes through Cygnus, Perseus, and Cassiopeia in the northern hemisphere, and Centaurus, Crux, and Sagittarius in the southern hemisphere. When you look at the Milky Way through binoculars or a telescope, you can see that it is made up of countless stars, seemingly packed close together. We also call our star system the Milky Way Galaxy, or just the galaxy. It has a spiral shape, with star-studded "arms" curving out from a dense bulge of stars in the middle.

MILKY WAY MYTHS
In the mythology of the Aztecs of Mexico, the Milky Way was identified with Mixcoatl, the cloud-serpent god. In ancient Egypt and India, it was seen as the celestial mirror of rivers like the Nile and Ganges. The Greeks believed it was a stream of milk from the breast of the goddess Hera, wife of Zeus the ruler of the gods.

ANATOMY OF THE GALAXY
Our galaxy is a vast system of around 500 billion stars. It measures 100,000 light-years across, but for the most part is only about 2,000 light-years thick. The spiral arms around the central bulge form the disk of the galaxy. There are two major arms, the Sagittarius and the Perseus, named from the constellations where they appear brightest. Between the two lies the Orion, or Local Arm, on which the Sun lies, 26,000 light-years from the galactic center.

Star-forming molecular clouds

Milky Way star clouds in Scorpius and Sagittarius

Orion arm

Location of our solar system

THE BACKBONE OF NIGHT
The Milky Way is best seen on clear, Moonless nights away from urban light pollution. Its brightest areas are most visible between June and September. The dark patches, or rifts, in the Milky Way are not starless regions, but areas in which dense dust clouds block the light from the stars behind them.

Central bulge of old red stars

Spiral arms are rich in young blue and white stars

Perseus arm

Outer arm

IN A SPIN

The Milky Way Galaxy spins around in space. If it didn't, it would soon collapse in on itself. Shifts in the spectra of stars scattered throughout the galaxy reveal that it is rotating. The stars on one side show a shift in spectral lines toward the blue, indicating that they are moving toward us. The stars on the other side show a red shift, showing that they are moving away. The same pattern shows up in other galaxies.

Blue shift on edge moving toward us

Red shift on edge moving away

Red and blue shifts in Andromeda Galaxy

*Sagittarius A**

Molecular ring

Radio lobe

HEART OF THE MILKY WAY

Radio and infrared studies have probed the gas- and dust-filled heart of the Milky Way Galaxy. At the very center is an intense radio source, Sagittarius A*, which is believed to be a massive black hole. Farther out are rings of magnetised gas (the radio lobe) and giant molecular clouds (the molecular ring). The molecular ring lies about 500 light-years from the center.

THE GALACTIC CENTER

This Chandra X-ray Observatory image shows the gas clouds and central cluster of stars in the very heart of the Milky Way Galaxy. The cluster contains nearly three million stars, many of them massive and very hot. It surrounds the Sagittarius A* black hole, which appears to have the mass of more than two million Suns. The black hole is dormant at present, but could become active if enough gas exists to feed it.

Massive stars close to central black hole

Glowing gas heated to 18 million°F (10 million°C)

Sagittarius arm

A typical spiral arm star orbits the center of the galaxy every 250 million or so years

Neighbors

In far southern skies, two misty patches can be seen in the constellations Tucana and Dorado. They are called the Large and Small Magellanic Clouds. They are not, as was once thought, clouds or nebulae in our own galaxy—instead, they are separate star systems, neighboring galaxies. The Large Magellanic Cloud lies just 160,000 light-years away, a mere stone's throw in space. It is small compared with our Galaxy and is irregular in shape, as is the Small Magellanic Cloud. The Magellanic Clouds and a number of smaller dwarf elliptical galaxies are not just neighbors of the Milky Way; they also come under its gravitational influence. In turn, the Milky Way and its satellites are bound by gravity into the Local Group, a family of galaxies some 3 million light-years across.

MAGELLAN'S CLOUDS
The Magellanic Clouds are named after Portuguese navigator Ferdinand Magellan (1480–1521). He commanded the first expedition to voyage around the world, which set out in 1519. He was one of the first Europeans to see the clouds and probably used them to navigate.

Small Magellanic Cloud

Large Magellanic Cloud

THE LOCAL GROUP
The Milky Way and its satellite galaxies form part of a much larger collection of galaxies called the Local Group. This group also includes two more spiral galaxies in the constellations Andromeda and Triangulum. All the other galaxies are elliptical or irregular galaxies, and are very much smaller. In all there are more than 40 galaxies in the Local Group, bound loosely together by gravity. In turn, the group forms part of a much larger cluster of galaxies.

SATELLITE GALAXIES
The Large Magellanic Cloud is 30,000 light-years across, less than one-third the size of the Milky Way. It contains much the same mix of stars and gas as our own galaxy, but has no features like a central bulge or spiral arms. It does have a broad band of relatively old stars, and also vast star-forming regions, such as the Tarantula Nebula. This nebula is one of the biggest and brightest known, lit up by a cluster of young, hot, massive stars. The Small Magellanic Cloud is only a quarter as massive as the Large Cloud and lies slightly farther away, 190,000 light-years from Earth.

Milky Way Galaxy

Sagittarius Dwarf Elliptical

OUR CANNIBAL GALAXY
There are small galaxies even closer to us than the Large Magellanic Cloud. The Sagittarius Dwarf Elliptical lies 80,000 light-years away, hidden behind the dense gas clouds in the center of our galaxy and only discovered in 1994. It is surprising that this dwarf galaxy has not been pulled apart by the Milky Way as it orbits it. Large amounts of invisible dark matter are believed to be keeping the galaxy together.

Sculptor

IC 1613

NGC 6822

Fornax

Small Magellanic Cloud

Large Magellanic Cloud

Sagittarius

Ursa Mi...

Dra...

Milky Way

Carina

Leo I

Leo II

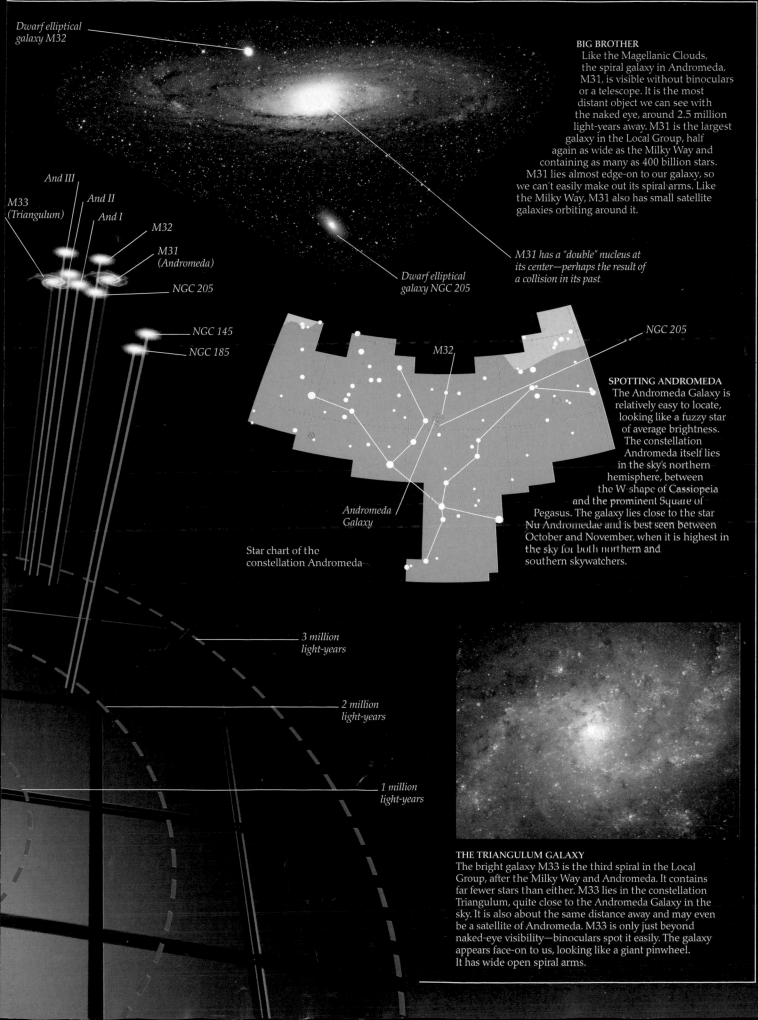

Dwarf elliptical galaxy M32

BIG BROTHER
Like the Magellanic Clouds, the spiral galaxy in Andromeda, M31, is visible without binoculars or a telescope. It is the most distant object we can see with the naked eye, around 2.5 million light-years away. M31 is the largest galaxy in the Local Group, half again as wide as the Milky Way and containing as many as 400 billion stars. M31 lies almost edge-on to our galaxy, so we can't easily make out its spiral arms. Like the Milky Way, M31 also has small satellite galaxies orbiting around it.

And III

And II

M33
(Triangulum)

And I

M32

M31
(Andromeda)

NGC 205

M31 has a "double" nucleus at its center—perhaps the result of a collision in its past

Dwarf elliptical galaxy NGC 205

NGC 145

NGC 185

NGC 205

M32

SPOTTING ANDROMEDA
The Andromeda Galaxy is relatively easy to locate, looking like a fuzzy star of average brightness. The constellation Andromeda itself lies in the sky's northern hemisphere, between the W shape of Cassiopeia and the prominent Square of Pegasus. The galaxy lies close to the star Nu Andromedae and is best seen between October and November, when it is highest in the sky for both northern and southern skywatchers.

Andromeda
Galaxy

Star chart of the constellation Andromeda

3 million light-years

2 million light-years

1 million light-years

THE TRIANGULUM GALAXY
The bright galaxy M33 is the third spiral in the Local Group, after the Milky Way and Andromeda. It contains far fewer stars than either. M33 lies in the constellation Triangulum, quite close to the Andromeda Galaxy in the sky. It is also about the same distance away and may even be a satellite of Andromeda. M33 is only just beyond naked-eye visibility—binoculars spot it easily. The galaxy appears face-on to us, looking like a giant pinwheel. It has wide open spiral arms.

Galaxies galore

THE MILKY WAY AND THE OTHER GALAXIES that make up the
Local Group occupy only a tiny region of space, a few million
light-years across. Scattered throughout the rest of space,
across tens of billions of light-years, are tens of billions of other
galaxies. Many are spiral in shape, like the Milky Way and the
Andromeda Galaxy. Many are oval, or elliptical, and others
have no regular shape at all. Some galaxies are dwarfs, with
maybe less than a million stars, but others are giants with
hundreds of billions. Occasionally, galaxies create
spectacular celestial fireworks as they crash
into one another. Astronomers don't know
exactly when galaxies started to form,
but it was probably less than
2 billion years after the
universe itself was born.

COLLIDING GALAXIES
Typically, adjacent galaxies are 10 galaxy
diameters apart. From time to time they
crash into one another. Usually, it is not
the individual stars that collide but the
vast gas clouds inside the galaxies. The
crashing together of the clouds triggers
off bouts of furious star formation,
known as starbursts.

*Stars are flung out of both
galaxies during collision*

*Elliptical galaxies classified
E0–E9 in order of increasing
ellipticity*

*Spiral galaxy
NGC 2207*

Elliptical galaxies (E)

Spiral galaxies (S)

Barred spiral galaxies (SB)

*Spirals and
barred spirals
classified Sa–Sc
and SBa–SBc,
depending on
the structure of
their arms*

Colliding galaxies
NGC 2207 and IC 2163

HUBBLE'S TUNING FORK
Galaxy pioneer Edwin Hubble
devised the method astronomers use
to classify galaxies. He divided up
regular galaxies into ellipticals (E),
spirals (S), and barred spirals (SB),
according to their shape, in his
so-called tuning-fork diagram.

*Starburst
region—a vast
stellar nursery*

IRREGULAR GALAXIES
Galaxies with no particular shape are classed
as irregulars. They are rich in gas and dust, and
have many young stars with plenty of star-
forming regions. The Magellanic Clouds
are irregulars, as is M82 in Ursa Major
(left). M82 is crossed by prominent
dark dust lanes and is undergoing
a massive burst of star
formation.

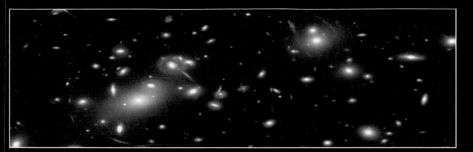

All galaxies interact with one another. Gravity binds them loosely together into small groups, like the Local Group, or often into much bigger clusters. The nearest big group is the Virgo Cluster, which spans a region of space about 10 million light-years across and contains more than 2,000 galaxies. In turn, the Milky Way and the Virgo Cluster form part of a much bigger supercluster. Strings of superclusters make up the large-scale structure of the universe.

Galaxy cluster Abell 2218

*Stars orbit at many
different angles*

*Elliptical galaxies contain
old yellow stars*

ELLIPTICAL GALAXIES

Elliptical, or ball-shaped, galaxies include the smallest and largest galaxies. The biggest may be up to a million light-years across. Giant ellipticals like M87 (right) are found in the heart of galaxy clusters. Ellipticals vary in shape from spherical to flattened oval. They are made up mainly of old stars and lack the gas to support much star formation.

*Collision compresses
gas clouds and triggers
bursts of star formation*

*Jet emerging
from galaxy core*

*Spiral galaxy
IC 2163*

*Larger galaxy's gravity
distorts smaller galaxy*

*Silhouetted dust lane
in NGC 2207*

LENTICULAR GALAXIES

Some galaxies seem to be a cross between spiral and elliptical galaxies. They are termed lenticular, or lens-shaped. Lenticular galaxies appear to be spirals without the spiral arms. They have a central bulge of old stars like spirals, and there are some young stars in the narrow surrounding disk, but they have no vast star-forming regions.

Lenticular galaxy NGC 2787

HOW FAR?

Astronomers can measure the distance to some galaxies by using Cepheid variables. The period over which Cepheid stars vary in brightness relates directly to their true brightness. From their true brightness and their apparent brightness in the sky, their distance can easily be calculated. Edwin Hubble (left) was first to use this method, calculating the distance to the Andromeda Galaxy in 1923.

Quasars and other active galaxies

LOOKING AT QUASARS
A former assistant to Edwin Hubble, US astronomer Allan Sandage (born 1926) helped discover quasars. In 1960, he linked radio source 3C48 with a faint starlike object but could not explain its spectrum. It was three years before 3C48 was identified as a quasar with a large red shift.

MOST GALAXIES GIVE OUT THE ENERGY of hundreds of billions of stars shining together, but some give out much more. We call these active galaxies, and they include radio galaxies, quasars, blazars, and Seyfert galaxies. Quasars are perhaps the most intriguing of active galaxies. Their name is short for "quasi-stellar radio source," because they look like faint stars and give off radio waves. But quasars have enormous red shifts, and so must lie billions of light-years away, far beyond the stars. Powerful telescopes reveal that they are in fact galaxies with very bright centers. To be visible at such distances, quasars must be hundreds of times brighter than normal galaxies, but rapid changes in their brightness mean that most of their light must be generated in a region little larger than our system system. Today, astronomers think that quasars and other active galaxies get their energy from massive black holes at their centers.

RADIO GALAXIES
NGC 5128 in the constellation Centaurus is an elliptical galaxy cut in two by a dark band of obscuring dust. It houses a powerful radio source called Centaurus A, and is the nearest active galaxy to us, just 15 million light-years away. This picture combines optical, X-ray (blue) and radio (red and green) views of the central region. A halo of X-ray-emitting gas surrounds the galaxy and a jet shoots out from its center, billowing out into huge radio-emitting lobes.

Camera

Polished metal mirror assembly used to reflect and focus X-rays

Solar panels

STUDYING ACTIVE GALAXIES
Violent activity in the heart of active galaxies produces copious amounts of high-energy radiation such as X-rays and gamma rays. Satellites such as the Chandra X-ray Observatory (above) and the Compton Gamma Ray Observatory are used to study high-energy rays from space, because these rays are blocked by the atmosphere.

Faint spiral arms 36,000 light-years across

Ring of intense starbirth around core

Bright core powered by black hole

Seyfert galaxy NGC 7742

SEYFERT GALAXIES
Some spiral galaxies have particularly bright centers and are classed as Seyfert galaxies after US astronomer Carl Seyfert, who first noticed them in 1943. They are now thought to be closer and less powerful versions of quasars. About one in 10 large spiral galaxies appear to be Seyferts, and our own Milky Way may become one in time.

DISTANT QUASARS
The Hubble Space Telescope has spotted this quasar in the constellation Sculptor, emitting radiation as visible light. The quasar's powerful energy emission is fueled by a collision between two galaxies—the remains of one spiral ring lie just below the quasar itself. The quasar lies 3 billion light-years away—a much closer star shines just above it.

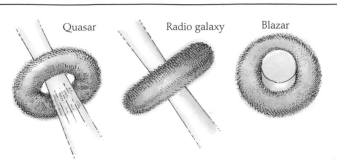

Quasar   Radio galaxy   Blazar

Intergalactic gas emits radio waves as jet slams into it

Jets billow out to form a lobe as they meet intergalactic gas

Quasar jets can travel at almost the speed of light

SAME ENGINE, DIFFERENT VIEWS
Astronomers believe that the various kinds of active galaxy are views of the same basic black-hole-driven "engine" from different angles. For example, quasars and Seyferts are views of the brilliant accretion disk. Radio galaxies show a side-on view, with the disk completely hidden from view, while blazars appear when we are looking right down the jet into the core.

UNDERSTANDING ACTIVE GALAXIES
The "engine" that powers every active galaxy has a distinctive structure. In the heart of the galaxy is a huge torus (ring) of gas, dust, and stars. A black hole lies in the center of the ring, surrounded by a spiraling disk of gas and dust that feeds into the black hole. The disk is searing hot and emits radiation and subatomic particles. These get caught up in powerful magnetic fields and ejected along the rotation axis as high-energy jets.

Material in disk is heated up by friction and gravity, emitting brilliant light and X-rays

Accretion disk is fueled by gas clouds and stars

Flattened accretion disk of material spiraling onto black hole

Supermassive black holes are produced by collapsing gas clouds in the center of galaxies

Central black hole weighs millions or billions of solar masses

Black hole's intense magnetic field drives jets of particles and radiation out from poles

Stars straying too close to black hole are torn to pieces

Dense ring of gas and dust surrounds central engine

Radio lobes are much farther away in reality

SUPERMASSIVE BLACK HOLES
This image reveals a giant black hole blowing bubbles of gas. Powerful jets are creating a glowing shell where they meet surrounding gas. It now seems most galaxies may have supermassive black holes at their cores.

A universe of life

EXTREMES OF LIFE
Scientists used to think that life could only arise in mild conditions like those on Earth's surface, but recent discoveries of creatures in extreme environments have changed their minds. Creatures even thrive on the deep-sea floor around black smokers—volcanic vents spewing out sulfur-laden water at 660°F (350°C).

Crab on a black smoker

OUR PLANET TEEMS WITH LIFE in extraordinary variety, but we know of no other place in the solar system or even in the universe where life exists. Surely there must be other life "out there." There are billions of stars like the Sun in our galaxy alone, and some of them must have planets capable of supporting life. And on some of these worlds, intelligent life should arise, capable of communicating across space. Since the 1960s, various projects have been set up to search for extraterrestrial intelligence (SETI) using radio telescopes. It seems likely that aliens would use radio waves of some sort to communicate, just as we do.

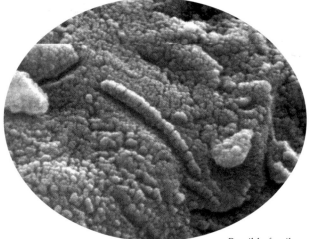

Possible fossil bacteria in Martian meteorite

LIFE IN THE SOLAR SYSTEM?
Mars has long been considered as a place where life of some sort might exist, either now or in the past. The planet is inhospitable to life now, but it probably had a more suitable climate long ago. If life gained a foothold at that time, it could have left fossils in the Martian soil. In 1996, NASA scientists thought they had found traces of ancient life in a meteorite from Mars but others are unconvinced.

HARBINGERS OF LIFE
Many carbon-based, organic molecules have been found in the gas clouds that exist between the stars. There are even simple amino acids, which are essential building blocks for life. This suggests that life might be common in the universe. It could be spread through solar systems by the most primitive of celestial bodies—the comets.

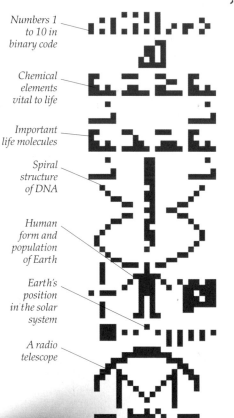

Numbers 1 to 10 in binary code

Chemical elements vital to life

Important life molecules

Spiral structure of DNA

Human form and population of Earth

Earth's position in the solar system

A radio telescope

TALKING TO ALIENS
The only message mankind has so far deliberately sent to aliens was transmitted in digital form as a set of 1,679 on-off pulses. This number is the result of multiplying two prime numbers, 23 and 73, and the message becomes clear when laid out in 73 rows of 23 columns. With black squares for 1s and white squares for 0s, a pattern or pictogram is produced that forms a message.

ARECIBO CALLING
The message (left) was transmitted from the huge Arecibo radio telescope in 1974. It was beamed at a globular cluster of 300,000 stars, increasing the possibility of reaching intelligent life. But the signal won't reach its target for another 25,000 years.

INTERSTELLAR MESSAGES
The *Pioneer 10* and *11* and *Voyager 1* and *2* space probes are now winging their way out of the solar system carrying messages for aliens. The Pioneers carry pictorial plaques; the Voyagers have gold record disks on which typical sights and sounds of Earth are recorded.

THE CHANCES OF LIFE
US radio astronomer Frank Drake (born 1930) pioneered the use of radio telescopes to listen for signals from aliens. He also devised an equation (left) that estimates how many advanced civilizations within our galaxy should be able and willing to communicate with us. Unfortunately, we still don't know enough about our universe to use the Drake Equation properly.

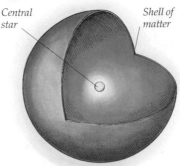

Central star

Shell of matter

SIGNS OF INTELLIGENCE
US physicist Freeman Dyson has suggested that an advanced civilization would remodel its corner of the universe, perhaps building a huge sphere around its star to trap energy. We could detect civilizations by looking for distinctive emissions from these "Dyson spheres."

WHAT MIGHT THEY BE LIKE?
It is almost impossible to guess what alien life would be like, but biologists can make educated guesses based on the principle of evolution. Simply put, this means that any creature must be well-suited to its environment in order to survive and pass on its characteristics to another generation. Using this principle, we can imagine viable aliens like this low-browsing herbivore from Epsilon Reticuli b.

Neck can retract and extend

Vibrating "hairs" detect sounds

Bristles insulate and protect the body

Eyes and a chemical-detecting nose—these are important senses in any environment

Defensive spikes

Armored hindquarters

Six walking legs with seven claws on each. Four limbs and five digits are nothing special

Our alien has an exoskeleton—it evolved from insectlike creatures

Specialized digging claw for raking tough plants out of soil

Mandibles crop and chop food against comblike teeth

CULTURE SHOCK
Some people believe that aliens are already visiting Earth and making contact with humans, but most think we have yet to make our first contact with alien intelligence. If and when that happens, the impact on humankind will be enormous. The clash in physical form and culture would be infinitely more shocking than when Columbus first met Native Americans in 1472 (left), and could be as damaging for our species as it was for the Native Americans.

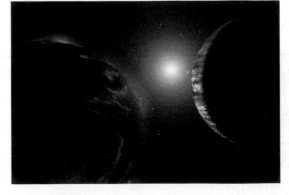

EPSILON RETICULI
The hypothetical alien above comes from a moon of the giant planet Epsilon Reticuli b, about 60 light-years from Earth. The planet, discovered in 2000, orbits its star just 20 percent farther out than Earth orbits the Sun. The star Epsilon Reticuli itself seems to be a Sunlike star just starting to evolve into its red giant phase.

Window on the universe

As we look out from Earth, we look into the universe. In the daytime, the Sun drowns out the light from more distant stars. At night, we see these as pinpricks of light against the dark backdrop of space. Earth's sky is divided into 88 constellations, or star patterns, that help us find our way around the sky. These two maps will help you identify the constellations. The first shows stars visible from Earth's northern hemisphere, and the second those that can be seen from the southern hemisphere. Over the course of the year, as Earth orbits the Sun, different stars become visible.

RECOGNIZING CONSTELLATIONS

Some constellations are easy to spot in the night sky. Others can be recognized from just a few stars in the full constellation. Seven stars in the back and tail of Ursa Major, the Great Bear, are easy to see. They are known as The Big Dipper.

The Big Dipper in the night sky

Position of The Big Dipper in Ursa Major

NORTHERN HEMISPHERE STARS
One point in the sky never moves. This fixed point is known as the celestial pole. In the northern hemisphere, Polaris (also called the North Star) is almost exactly on the celestial north pole. It is the brightest star in the constellation of Ursa Minor.

USING THE MAPS
Turn the book so that the name of the current month is at the bottom. Northern hemisphere observers should face south to see the stars in the map's lower part and center. Those using the southern hemisphere map should face north.

This view of Taurus shows the bright star Aldebaran at upper left, just above the fainter Hyades star cluster; on the right is the Pleiades star cluster.

The Double Cluster, two dense groupings of hundreds of stars (left and right of center), can be seen in the constellation of Perseus.

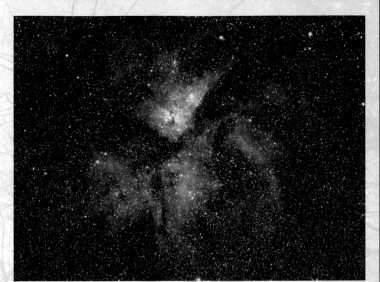

The path of the Milky Way is broadest and brightest in the constellations of Sagittarius and Scorpius. As we look at it, we are gazing into the heart of the Milky Way Galaxy from near the inner edge of one of its spiral arms.

SOUTHERN HEMISPHERE STARS
Unlike the northern hemisphere sky, the southern hemisphere sky does not have a North Star. The celestial south pole (the fixed point around which the stars in the southern sky seem to rotate) is just a blank area of sky.

The Carina Nebula in the constellation of Carina is one of the largest and brightest of all nebulae. It is illuminated by stars embedded within its gas and dust.

The white dotted line represents the ecliptic—the path of the Sun across the sky

The light-blue areas represent the Milky Way—the stars of our galaxy's disk, which appear as a dense band of stars across the night sky

The red lines work like latitude and longitude on Earth, helping to pinpoint objects in the sky

JULY
JUNE
AUGUST
MAY
DRACO
HERCULES
CORONA BOREALIS
LYRA
BOÖTES
SEPTEMBER
CYGNUS
OPHIUCHUS
SERPENS CAPUT
CANES VENATICI
APRIL
SAGITTA
AQUILA
SERPENS CAUDA
VIRGO
DELPHINUS
SCUTUM
LIBRA
COMA BERENICES
CEPHEUS
EQUULEUS
SCORPIUS
LUPUS
CORVUS
CRATER
URSA MAJOR
LACERTA
AQUARIUS
CAPRICORNUS
CORONA AUSTRALIS
SAGITTARIUS
PISCIS AUSTRINUS
CETUS
NORMA
ARA
TELESCOPIUM
CENTAURUS
LEO
LEO MINOR
MARCH
PEGASUS
GRUS
INDUS
PAVO
OCTANS
APUS
TRIANGULUM AUSTRALE
CRUX
SEXTANS
ANTLIA
CHAMAELEON
Carina Nebula
TUCANA
HYDRUS
MENSA
VOLANS
CARINA
VELA
CASSIOPEIA
ANDROMEDA
SCULPTOR
PHOENIX
DORADO
RETICULUM
HOROLOGIUM
PICTOR
PUPPIS
PYXIS
HYDRA
CANCER
FEBRUARY
PISCES
FORNAX
Fornax Cluster
COLUMBA
CANIS MAJOR
CANIS MINOR
GEMINI
ARIES
CETUS
LEPUS
Sirius
MONOCEROS
LYNX
ERIDANUS
ORION
TAURUS
AURIGA
PERSEUS
NOVEMBER
OCTOBER
DECEMBER
JANUARY

The Fornax Cluster of galaxies, made mostly of elliptical galaxies, is located in the constellation of Fornax.

Sirius (center right) in the constellation of Canis Major is the brightest star in the entire sky. To the left is the distinctive constellation of Orion, the hunter (head down).

Discovery timeline

THE UNIVERSE IS ABOUT 13.75 BILLION YEARS OLD. It formed in the Big Bang explosion that signaled the start of all space, time, energy, and matter, and ever since it has been expanding, cooling, and changing. Humans have studied the universe for thousands of years. We first analyzed the movements of the heavenly bodies by eye, then explored these bodies more closely with telescopes and space probes. Recently, we have pieced together the story of the whole universe, from its beginning to the present day.

Saturn's rings, first described correctly in 1655

The Crab Nebula, the remnant of a supernova seen in 1054

c. 4000 BCE
The Egyptians, Chaldeans, and Hindus name bright stars and form them into constellations. Twelve of these are the zodiac constellations.

c. 2000 BCE
Lunar and solar calendars are introduced.

550 BCE
Pythagoras, a Greek mathematician, suggests that the Sun, Moon, Earth, and planets are spherical.

360 BCE
The Greek philosopher Aristotle proposes that the planets are stuck in rotating crystal spheres and that all stars are the same distance away. He states that the universe is changeless and made from a combination of fire, water, earth, and air.

290 BCE
In Greece, the astronomer Aristarchus uses lunar eclipse timings to show that the distance between the Earth and the Moon is equal to about 31 times Earth's width, and that the Moon is just over one-quarter the size of Earth.

150 BCE
Hipparchus measures the length of the year to an accuracy of 6 minutes. He catalogs the position and brightness of stars, and states that the Sun's orbit around Earth is elliptical after observing that Earth's seasons are of unequal length.

c. 130 CE
Ptolemy writes *The Almagest*, which summarizes the astronomical knowledge of the time, including a list of bright stars in 48 constellations.

c. 800
Arab astronomers refine astronomical knowledge, including defining the ecliptic (the path of the Sun across the sky) and the orbital periods of the Sun, Moon, and planets.

1054
Chinese astronomers record a supernova in the constellation of Taurus. The remnants of this are seen today as the Crab Nebula.

1252
In Spain, King Alphonso X commissions the Alphonsine Tables, which accurately list planetary positions.

1420
Mongol ruler Ulugh Beg builds an observatory in Samarkand (now part of Uzbekistan). His catalog of naked-eye star positions is the first since that of Hipparchus.

1543
Nicolaus Copernicus, a Polish astronomer, publishes *On the Revolution of the Heavenly Spheres*. His book signals the end of the idea of an Earth-centered universe.

1572
Danish nobleman Tycho Brahe observes a supernova in Cassiopeia and shows that it lies beyond the Moon. Stars are thus not a fixed distance away, but changeable objects existing in "space."

1596
Tycho Brahe finishes 20 years of highly accurate planetary observations.

1609
German astronomer Johannes Kepler devises two laws. First, that planets have elliptical orbits, with the Sun at one focus of the ellipse. Second, that a planet moves fastest when close to the Sun, and slower when farther away.

1610
In Italy, Galileo Galilei publishes the results of his telescopic studies in *Siderius Nuncius*. These show that the Moon is mountainous, Jupiter has four Moons, and the Sun is spotty and rotates. Galileo states that the phases of Venus indicate that the Sun, not Earth, lies at the solar system's center and declares that the Milky Way is made up of a myriad of stars that are merely very distant suns.

1619
Johannes Kepler devises his third law, which describes the mathematical relationship between a planet's orbital period and its average distance from the Sun.

1655
Christiaan Huygens, a Dutch mathematician and astronomer, correctly describes Saturn's ring system and discovers Saturn's moon, Titan.

1675
In Denmark, Ole Römer uses the eclipse times of Jupiter's moons to measure the speed of light.

1686
English astronomer Edmond Halley shows that "his" comet is periodic and part of the solar system. It sweeps past the Sun every 76 years.

1687
Isaac Newton, an English physicist, publishes his theory of gravity in *Principia*. It explains why the planets orbit the Sun and gives a value for the mass of the Sun and Earth.

1761 and 1769
Astronomers observe the transits of Venus across the face of the Sun, which are used to calculate an accurate value for the distance between the Sun and Earth.

1769
The first predicted return of a comet (Halley's) proves that the laws of gravity extend at least to the edge of the solar system.

1781
William Herschel discovers the planet Uranus using a home-built telescope in his backyard in Bath, England.

1784
A list of 103 "fuzzy" nebulae is drawn up by Frenchman Charles Messier.

1785
William Herschel describes the shape of the Milky Way Galaxy.

Willaim Herschel discovered Uranus in 1781

1801
Giuseppe Piazzi, an Italian monk, discovers Ceres, the first asteroid.

1815
Joseph von Fraunhofer, a German optician, maps the dark lines in the solar spectrum.

1838
German astronomer Friedrich Bessel calculates that the star 61 Cygni is 11 light-years away. It is the first non-solar stellar distance measured.

1840
In the US, the Moon is photographed by scientist John W. Draper. It is the first use of photography to record astronomical data.

1846
Neptune is discovered by using Newton's laws of gravitation to predict how it disturbs the orbit of Uranus.

1864
In England, William Huggins uses a spectrometer to show that comets contain carbon and that stars consist of the same chemical elements as Earth.

1879
Austrian mathematician and physicist Josef Stefan realizes that the total energy radiated by a star is proportional to its surface area and surface temperature. Stephan's Law allows stellar sizes to be estimated.

1890
About 30 stellar distances have now been measured, and astronomers are starting to do stellar statistics.

1900
New knowledge of the radioactive decay of elements leads to the realization that Earth is over one billion years old and that the Sun has been shining for a similar time period.

1905
Albert Einstein proposes that $E = mc^2$, meaning that energy (E) can be produced by destroying mass (m). This is the breakthrough in understanding energy generation in stars.

1910
By plotting stellar surface temperature and stellar luminosity, Ejnar Hertzsprung, a Dane, and Henry Russell, an American, find that there are only two main groups of stars: "dwarfs," such as the Sun; and "giants," which are much larger.

1912
American astronomer Henrietta Leavitt finds that the time periods between the maximum brightnesses of Cepheid giant stars are related to their luminosities. This relationship can be used to measure stellar distances.

1917
The 100-inch (2.5-meter) Hooker Telescope on Mount Wilson, California, is used for the first time. It detects Cepheid stars in the Andromeda Nebula, revealing that Andromeda is a galaxy. It is the first galaxy known to exist aside from our own Milky Way.

Charged-coupled device (CCD), 1980

1920
American Harlow Shapley finds that, far from being at the center of the Milky Way, the Sun is actually two-thirds of the way toward the edge.

1925
Cecilia Payne-Gaposchkin, an Anglo-American astronomer, shows that 75 percent of a star's mass is hydrogen.

Cecilia Payne-Gaposchkin, 1925

1926
English astrophysicist Arthur Eddington finds that for most of a star's life its luminosity is directly dependent on its mass.

1927
American Edwin Hubble shows that the universe is expanding. The more distant the galaxy, the faster it is moving away.

1930
Pluto is discovered by American Clyde Tombaugh.

1931
US physicist Karl Jansky detects radio waves from the Milky Way's center.

1931
Georges Lemaître, a Belgian priest and scientist, suggests that all matter in the universe started as a single, highly condensed sphere. This exploded in a "Big Bang" and has been getting larger ever since.

1939
German-American physicist Hans Bethe shows how destroying hydrogen and producing helium yields stellar energy.

1955
Englishman Fred Hoyle and his German colleague Martin Schwarzschild show how helium changes into carbon and oxygen in giant stars and how higher elements like cobalt and iron are made when massive stars explode as supernovae.

Eris, reclassified in 2006 and 2008

1963
The first quasar is identified—object 3C48.

1965
Americans Arno Penzias and Robert Wilson discover cosmic microwave background radiation—remnant radiation from the Big Bang.

1967
Belfast-born Jocelyn Bell-Burnell discovers the first pulsar.

1971
The first black hole Cygnus X-1 is discovered due to its effect on its companion star.

1980
In the US, Vera Rubin finds that many galaxies contain dark matter that affects their spin speed.

1980
US cosmologist Alan Guth modifies the Big Bang theory. He introduces "inflation," whereby the very young universe expands from the size of a proton to the size of a watermelon in an instant.

1980
Charged-coupled devices (the electronic chips in digital cameras) are used in astronomy. They are nearly 100-percent efficient at converting light into electronic signals.

1992
The first Kuiper Belt object is discovered by Englishman David Jewitt and Jane Luu, a Vietnamese-American.

1992
The first discovery of exoplanets—planets orbiting stars other than the Sun. They are detected around the pulsar PSR 1257+12.

1995
The first exoplanet orbiting an ordinary main sequence star, 51 Pegasi, is discovered.

2006
The category of dwarf planets is introduced after the discovery of Eris in 2005. Pluto is reclassified as a dwarf planet.

2008
Eris and Pluto are to known as plutoids—dwarf planets orbiting the Sun beyond Neptune.

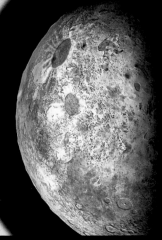

Find out more

BOOKS ARE A GREAT WAY TO FIND OUT ABOUT THE UNIVERSE, but you may want to be more than an armchair astronomer. Start by looking up and exploring the sky for yourself, watching the view change month by month. By joining a society of other amateur astronomers, you'll soon find your way around the sky. Take a visit to an observatory where astronomers tackle today's unanswered questions or have helped to unravel mysteries in the past. Museums and space centers tell the story of space exploration. You could even time your visit to coincide with the launch of a spacecraft on a new voyage of discovery.

Tanegashima Space Center, Japan

SPACE CENTERS
Some space centers have public viewing areas where you can watch the launch of a space shuttle or a rocket, or see space engineers preparing the next generation of spacecraft. Websites for centers such as Tanegashima, Japan, and the Kennedy Space Center, in Florida, give details of upcoming launches.

RADIO TELESCOPES
Unlike optical telescopes, radio telescopes are sited on low-lying ground and are more accessible. Telescopes such as Jodrell Bank, UK, Parkes in Australia, and the Green Bank in West Virginia, USA, welcome visitors. You can get up close to the telescopes, and learn about their use in the visitor centers.

Parkes Radio Telescope, Australia

Places to visit

KENNEDY SPACE CENTER, FLORIDA
This space complex sent men to the Moon in the 1960s, and it has launched astronauts aboard the Space Shuttle since 1981. Relive space history as you tour the exhibits, ask a current astronaut a question, and watch the preparations for a future launch.

MAUNA KEA OBSERVATORIES, HAWAII
The summit of the dormant Mauna Kea volcano is home to 13 working telescopes including the Kecks, the largest telescopes in the world. The twin Kecks stand eight stories tall and have mirrors 33 ft (10 m) in diameter. Regular stargazing sessions and tours of the summit are available.

ROSE CENTER FOR EARTH AND SPACE, AMERICAN MUSEUM OF NATURAL HISTORY, NEW YORK CITY
This center features Scales of the Universe, a walkway that illustrates the vastness of the universe, and the Hayden Planetarium, the world's largest virtual-reality simulator.

OBSERVATORIES
Today's world-class optical observatories are built on mountaintop locations far from inhabited areas. Most observatories are far too remote to visit, but some situated at lower altitudes have public access programs. You can look around the observatory site and a few observatories will even let you gaze through a telescope. Among those you can visit are Yerkes, near Chicago; Greenwich, in London, UK; and Meudon, near Paris, France.

Yerkes Observatory, US

PLANETARIUMS AND MUSEUMS

A visit to a planetarium—an indoor theater where images of space are projected above your head—will help you become familiar with the night sky. As the lights dim, a universe of stars is revealed on the planetarium's domed ceiling. Get to know the constellations before being transported across space to see planets and stars in close-up. Many science museums also exhibit telescopes, spacecraft, spacesuits, and rocks that have crash-landed on Earth from space.

Mexico City's planetarium

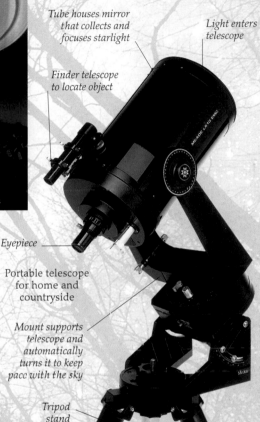

Tube houses mirror that collects and focuses starlight

Light enters telescope

Finder telescope to locate object

Eyepiece

Portable telescope for home and countryside

Mount supports telescope and automatically turns it to keep pace with the sky

Tripod stand

HOME SKYWATCHING

On a clear, Moonless, and cloud-free night you can look out from Earth and see the universe for yourself. From a typical city you will be able to pick out around 300 stars using your eyes alone, and 10 times more will be visible from a dark, rural location. Binoculars reveal still more stars, as well as adding clarity to your view of objects such as the Moon and star clusters. Telescopes bring the objects even closer, making them appear brighter and larger.

Viewing with binoculars

JOINING A GROUP OR SOCIETY

Skywatching with others is fun, and also a great way to learn. National societies and associations publish journals and hold meetings for members. You can also find local amateur astronomical organizations in many towns and cities. Some of these have their own telescopes and hold regular observing sessions. Professional astronomers often visit these groups to pass on the latest discoveries and research findings. If you can't commit to regular meetings, look out for special events such as eclipse-watching.

Glossary

ACTIVE GALAXY A galaxy emitting an exceptional amount of energy, much of which comes from a central supermassive black hole.

ASTEROID A small rocky body orbiting the Sun. Most asteroids orbit in the Asteroid Belt between Mars and Jupiter.

ASTRONOMY The study of everything in space, including space itself.

ATMOSPHERE The layer of gas around a planet or moon, or beyond a star's photosphere, that is held in place by gravity.

AURORA The colorful light display of glowing gas in the upper atmosphere above a planet's polar regions.

BARRED SPIRAL GALAXY A galaxy with spiral arms that curl out from the ends of a bar-shaped nucleus.

BIG BANG The explosion that created the universe. The origin of space, time, and matter.

BINARY STAR A pair of stars, each of which revolves around the overall center of mass of the two-star system.

BLACK HOLE A compact region of space where mass has collapsed and whose gravity stops anything, including light, from escaping. Some black holes result from the collapse of a single star. Supermassive black holes at the center of galaxies are the result of a very large amount of mass collapsing.

BRIGHTNESS A measure of the light of a star as seen from Earth (*see* Luminosity).

BROWN DWARF A star with too little mass to start the nuclear fusion process that powers a normal star.

CEPHEID A type of variable star whose brightness changes in a regular way over time as the star alternately expands and contracts.

CLUSTER A group of stars or galaxies that are gravitationally bound together in space.

COMET A small body of snow, ice, and dust known as a nucleus that orbits the Sun beyond the planets. A comet traveling close to the Sun develops a large head and tails.

Comet McNaught, 2007

Barringer Crater, Arizona

CONSTELLATION One of the 88 areas of Earth's sky whose bright stars form an imaginary pattern.

CORONA The outermost region of the Sun's atmosphere.

COSMOLOGY The study of the universe as a whole, and its origin and evolution.

CRATER A bowl-shaped hollow in the surface of a planet or moon. An impact crater is formed by the impact of a meteorite; a volcanic crater is where a volcano ejects material.

DARK ENERGY An unknown form of energy that makes up 73 percent of the universe.

DARK MATTER Matter that makes up 23 percent of the universe. It does not emit energy, but its gravity affects its surroundings.

DOUBLE STAR Two stars that appear very close together in Earth's sky, but which are in reality physically separate.

DWARF PLANET A near-spherical body orbiting the Sun as part of a belt of objects.

ECLIPSE An effect due to the passage of one space body into the shadow of another. In a solar eclipse, the Moon covers the Sun and its shadow falls on Earth. In a lunar eclipse, the Moon moves into Earth's shadow.

ECLIPTIC The yearly path followed by the Sun in Earth's sky.

ELECTROMAGNETIC RADIATION The energy waves given off by space objects. These include light, X-rays, and radio and infrared wavelengths.

ELLIPTICAL GALAXY A round- or elliptical-shaped galaxy.

EXTRASOLAR PLANET (EXOPLANET) A planet orbiting a star other than the Sun.

EXTRATERRESTRIAL LIFE A life form not originating on Earth. No extraterrestrial life has so far been discovered.

GALAXY A grouping of a vast number of stars, gas, and dust held together by gravity. The Sun is one of the stars in the Milky Way Galaxy.

GAS GIANT A large planet that consists predominantly of hydrogen and helium, which are in gaseous form at the planet's visible surface. Jupiter, Saturn, Uranus, and Neptune are the gas giants of the solar system.

GLOBULAR CLUSTER A near-spherical cluster of old stars found predominantly in the halo of a galaxy.

GRAVITY A force of attraction found throughout the universe.

HERTZSPRUNG-RUSSELL (H-R) DIAGRAM A diagram in which stars are plotted according to their luminosity and surface temperature, and which shows different classes of stars, such as giants and dwarfs.

INTERSTELLAR MATERIAL Gas and dust between the stars in a galaxy.

IRREGULAR GALAXY A galaxy with no obvious shape or structure.

Neptune, a gas giant

KUIPER BELT The flattened belt of rock and ice bodies that orbit the Sun beyond Neptune.

LENTICULAR GALAXY A galaxy in the shape of a convex lens.

LIGHT-YEAR A unit of distance used outside the solar system. One light-year is the distance light travels in one year: 5.88 million million miles (9.46 million million km).

LOCAL GROUP The cluster of more than 40 galaxies that includes the Milky Way.

LUMINOSITY The total amount of energy emitted in one second by a star.

MAIN SEQUENCE STAR A star, such as the Sun, that shines steadily by converting hydrogen into helium. A category of stars on the Hertzsprung-Russell diagram.

MASS The amount of matter in an object.

METEOR A short-lived streak of light that is produced by a meteoroid (a tiny piece of a comet or asteroid) as it travels through Earth's atmosphere.

METEORITE A piece of asteroid (occasionally a piece of a comet, moon, or planet) that has traveled through space and lands on a planet or moon.

MILKY WAY The spiral-shaped galaxy that includes the Sun. It is also the name of the path of stars in Earth's night sky that is our view of the galaxy's disk of stars.

MOON A body orbiting a planet or asteroid. Also called a natural satellite. The Moon is Earth's satellite.

NEBULA A vast cloud of gas and dust in interstellar space (*see* Planetary nebula).

NEUTRON STAR An ultradense, compact star formed from the core of a star that explodes as a supernova.

NOVA A star that suddenly brightens at least a thousand-fold, and then fades back to normal brightness over the following months.

NUCLEAR FUSION The process that takes place within a star's core, whereby atomic nuclei join to form heavier atomic nuclei and energy is released.

NUCLEUS The body of a comet, the core of a galaxy, or the core of an atom.

OBSERVATORY A building or complex housing telescopes, from where observations of the universe are made. Sometimes used to describe a telescope orbiting Earth.

OORT CLOUD A sphere of more than a trillion comets surrounding the planetary part of the solar system.

Meteorite fragment

ORBIT The path taken by a natural or artificial body around another of greater mass.

PHOTOSPHERE The gaseous but visible outer surface of the Sun, or other star.

PLANET A massive round body that orbits a star and shines by that star's light.

PLANETARY NEBULA A late stage in the life of a star such as the Sun. A planetary nebula consists of a colorful glowing shell of gas ejected by the central star.

PROTOSTAR An early stage in the formation of a star. Gas is collapsing to form a star, but nuclear fusion has not started in the star's core.

PULSAR A rapidly rotating neutron star identified by the brief pulses of energy we receive as it spins.

QUASAR An active galaxy that is compact and extremely luminous.

RADIO GALAXY An active galaxy that is exceptionally luminous at radio wavelengths.

RED GIANT A large, red, luminous star—the late stage in the life of a star such as the Sun.

SATELLITE A natural body orbiting another more massive body, or an artificial body orbiting Earth.

SEYFERT GALAXY An active galaxy that is a spiral galaxy with an exceptionally luminous and compact nucleus.

SHOOTING STAR An everyday name for a meteor.

SOLAR CYCLE An 11-year period of varying solar activity, such as the production of sunspots.

SOLAR SYSTEM The Sun and all the bodies that orbit round it.

Cat's Eye Nebula (NGC 6543), a planetary nebula

SPACE The region beyond Earth's atmosphere and in which all bodies of the universe exist. Also used to describe the region between astronomical bodies.

SPECTRAL CLASS The classification of a star according to the lines in the star's spectrum. The main classes are known by the letters O, B, A, F, G, K, and M.

SPEED OF LIGHT The constant speed at which light and other electromagnetic radiation travels: 186,000 miles per second (299,792,458 meters per second).

SPIRAL GALAXY A disk-shaped galaxy with spiral arms that curl out from a dense central bulge of stars. The Milky Way is a spiral galaxy.

STAR A huge spinning sphere of very hot and very luminous gas that generates energy by nuclear reactions in its core.

SUNSPOT A dark, cool region on the visible surface of the Sun or another star.

SUPERCLUSTER A group of galaxy clusters. The Milky Way Galaxy belongs to the galaxy cluster known as the Local Group, which is one of the clusters in the Local Supercluster.

Spiral galaxy NGC 4414

SUPERGIANT A very large and very luminous star.

SUPERNOVA A massive star that has exploded and which is briefly up to a million times brighter than usual. The expanding cloud of debris is called a supernova remnant.

TELESCOPE An instrument that uses lenses or mirrors, or a combination of the two, to collect and focus light to form an image of a distant object. Some telescopes collect other wavelengths, such as radio and infrared.

TERRESTRIAL PLANETS The solar system's four rocky planets: Mercury, Venus, Earth, and Mars.

UNIVERSE Everything that exists: all the galaxies, stars, and planets, and the space in between, and all things on Earth.

VARIABLE STAR A star whose brightness varies over time by, for example, expanding and contracting, or erupting (*see* Cepheid *and* Nova).

WHITE DWARF An end-stage in the life of a star; a small, dim star that has stopped generating energy by nuclear reaction.

Index

Acknowledgments

Dorling Kindersley would like to thank: : Darren Naish and Mark Longworth for Epsilon Reticuli b Alien; Peter Bull for other artworks; Jonathan Brooks and Sarah Mills for additional research.

For this edition, the publisher would also like to thank: Carole Stott for assisting with the updates; Lisa Stock for editorial assistance, David Ekholm-JAlbum, Sunita Gahir, Susan Reuben, Susan St Louis, Lisa Stock, and Bulent Yusuf for the clip art; Sue Nicholson and Edward Kinsey for the wall chart; Monica Byles and Stewart J Wild for proofreading; Margaret Parrish for Americanization.

Picture credits:
The publisher would like to thank the following for their kind permission to reproduce their photographs:

(Key: a-above; b-below/bottom; c-center; f-far; l-left; r-right; t-top)

Agence France Presse: 52bl. **akg-images:** 39tr, 45br; Cameraphoto 40tl. **Alamy Images:** Classic Image 66b; Danita Delimont / Russell Gordon 69tc. **Anglo-Australian Observatory:** David Malin 51tr. **The Art Archive:** Musée du Louvre, Paris / Dagli Orti (A) 27cr. **Bridgeman Art Library, London / New York:** Archives Charmet 47br. **British Museum:** 6bl. © **CERN Geneva:** 2tr, 10bl. **Corbis:** 62bc; Lucien Aigner 14tl; Yann Arthus-Bertrand 8cl; Bettmann 3tl, 7tr, 12bl, 18tl, 32cl, 59br, 67cl; Araldo de Luca 20tl; Dennis di Cicco 40-41c; Paul Hardy 14clb; Charles & Josette Lenars 70tc; NASA 8clb, 39br; Michael Neveux 4cr, 6c; Robert Y. Ono 45bl; Enzo & Paolo Ragazzini 6bc; Roger Ressmeyer 4cl, 13tl, 17tr, 62cr, 68br, 68cl, 69bl; Paul A. Souders 29tr; Stapleton Collection 45cr; Brenda Tharp 53cla; Robert Yin 29br. **DK Images:** Natural History Museum, London 71cr. **European Space Agency:** 11crb; D. Ducros 17bl; ISO / ISOCAM / Alain Abergel 11br; NASA 40c. © **Stéphane Guisard:** 70bl. **Courtesy of JAXA:** 68tr. **Mary Evans Picture Library:** 8tl, 26bc, 27crb, 31br, 41cr, 56tl, 63bl; Alvin Correa 31br. **Galaxy Picture Library:** 25tl, 56cl, 57c, 57br, 59cra. **Getty Images:** Barros & Barros 12tl; Sean Hunter: 29cra. **Kobal Collection:** Universal 22c. **FLPA - Images of nature:** B. Borrell 22cb, 22crb. **NASA:** 2b, 2cl, 3c, 3tr, 5tr, 9c, 9bl (x6), 11tl, 16br, 17br, 18cl, 18c, 19tr, 23tr, 23ca, 23cr, 23br, 26, 27tr, 27br, 27br, 27l, 29cr, 30br, 31cr, 31ac, 33tr, 33bl, 35cra, 35bl, 35bc, 35ac, 37cr, 38-39c, 50-51b, 55br; Craig Attebery 35br; AURA / STScI 49tr; Boomerang Project 13c; Carnegie Mellon University 39cr; W.N. Colley and E. Turner (Princeton University), J.A. Tyson (Bell Labs, Lucent Technologies) 15cr; CXC / ASU/J 52c; ESA and The Hubble Heritage Team (STScI / AURA) 47bc; HST Comet Science Team 32bc; Institute of Space and Astronautical Sciences, Japan 21tr; JHUAPL 39tl, 39tc; JPL 8ca, 32c, 32bl, 33tc, 33cra, 33c, 33ac, 36clb, 36bc, 18bl, 66cla;

66tr, 70cr; JPL / University of Arizona 32-33; JSC 62cl; NASA HQ-GRIN 71cr; NOAO, ESA and The Hubble Heritage Team (STScI / AURA) 47tr; SOHO 20bl; Courtesy of SOHO / Extreme Ultraviolet Imaging Telescope (EIT) consortium 21bl; STScI 7bc, 9tr, 43tl, 48b, 49cr, 49br, 58-59c, 59tc, 59bl, 60cl, 60bl, 60br, 61br; STScI / COBE / DIRBE Science Team 8bl; TRW 60cr; Dr. Hal Weaver and T. Ed Smith (STScI) 40bl. **Musée de la Poste, Paris:** 37c. **National Maritime Museum:** 4tr, 7cra, 43bc; NOAA: OAR / National Undersea Research Program (NURP) 62tl. **NOAO / AURA / NSF:** N.A.Sharp 58; Pikaia: 2cra, 2crb, 4tl, 6-7, 9cl, 12bc, 14bl, 14-15, 15br, 24-25, 26tr, 27tc, 29tc, 30l, 31tr, 31cl, 36l, 37tc, 37bc, 37br, 44bl, 48tl, 49tl, 52cl, 53b, 56bl, 61c, 62bl, 62br, 64br, 65tr. **Vicent Peris (OAUV / PTeam), astrophotographer of the Astronomical Observatory of the University of Valencia (OAUV):** MAST, STScI, AURA, NASA - Image processed with PixInsight at OAUV. Based on observations made with the NASA / ESA Hubble Space Telescope, obtained at the Space Telescope Science Institute, which is operated by the Association of Universities for Research in Astronomy, Inc., under NASA contract NAS 5-26555. 71bl. **Photolibrary:** Corbis 64-71 (background). **Science Photo Library:** 10cl, 31bl, 31bl, 34br, 38bl; Michael Abbey 39bl; Estate of Francis Bello 60tl; Lawrence Berkeley Laboratory 15crb; Dr Eli Brinks 55tr; Celestial Image Co. 47c, 65bl; Luke Dodd 46bl; Bernhard Edmaier 28cl; Dr Fred Espenak 6-7, 8-9, 26bl; Mark Garlick 19tl, 43tr, 67br; D.Golimowski, S.Durrance & M. Clampin 49cl; Hale Observatories 52tr; David A Hardy 12-13, 36c, 51br; Harvard College

Observatory 19br, 43br; Jerry Lodriguss 64bl; Claus Lunau / FOCI / Bonnier Publications 41bl; Maddox, Sutherland, Efstathiou & Loveday 9br; Allan Morton / Dennis Milon 54bl; MPIA-HD, Birkle, Slawik 7cr, 57tc; NASA 13tr, 28bl, 44bc; National Optical Astonomy Observatories 21cra; Novosti Press Agency 41br; David Parker 67tc; Ludek Pesek 34cl; Detlev Van Ravenswaay 38cl; Royal Observatory, Edinburgh / AAO 46-47; Rev. Ronald Royer 20-21t; John Sanford 16bl, 42crb; Robin Scagell 52br; Jerry Schad 65tl; Dan Schechter 14cl; Dr Seth Shostak 63tl; Eckhard Slawik 64tr; Joe Tucciarone 54-55c.

Babak A. Tafreshi: 65br.

Wall chart
DK Images: Anglo-Australian Observatory, photography by David Malin fcra; London Planetarium (Mars), cra (Venus); Rough Guides tl; **NASA:** br (Chandra), cra (Earth), crb (star cluster); Finley Holiday Films bl; MSFC fcrb; **Science Photo Library:** Mark Garlick cl; NASA cla; Friedrich Saurer c; Detlev Van Ravenswaay clb.

All other images © Dorling Kindersley
For further information see:
www.dkimages.com

31901047129871